Helping Children Who Are Deaf

Family and community support for children who do not hear well

By Sandy Niemann,
Devorah Greenstein,
and Darlena David

Illustrated by Heidi Broner

The Hesperian Foundation
Berkeley, California, USA

First edition: March 2004.

Printed in the USA.

ISBN: 0-942364-44-9

Library of Congress Cataloging-in-Publication Data

Niemann, Sandy.

   Helping children who are deaf: family and community support for children who do not hear well / by Sandy Niemann, Devorah Greenstein, and Darlena David ; illustrated by Heidi Broner.-- 1st ed.

     p. cm. -- (Early assistance series for children with disabilities)

   Includes bibliographical references.

   ISBN 0-942364-44-9 (pbk.)

   1. Deaf children--means of communication. 2. Deaf children--Family relationships. 3. Deaf children--Services for. 4. Child development. I. Greenstein Devorah, 1944- II. David, Darlena. III. Title. IV. Series.

HV2391.N54 2004
362.4'25'083--dc22

Cover photograph:
by Devorah Greenstein, of a deaf boy and his father in Haiti.
The boy is using a sign he made up to describe
the bright light from a camera's flash.

Cover art: anonymous indigenous design, Panama.

The Hesperian Foundation
1919 Addison Street, Suite 304
Berkeley, California 94704, United States of America

Credits

Project coordinator:
Darlena David

Art coordination:
Sarah Wallis, Nicole Perez,
Devorah Greenstein

Design and production:
Sarah Wallis

Cover design:
Sarah Wallis

Additional writing:
Todd Jailer, Susan McCallister,
Nicole Perez, Tawnia Queen,
Sarah Shannon, Sarah Wallis

Research assistance:
Amina La Cour Mini, Nicole
Perez, Tawnia Queen, Rebecca
Ratcliff, Amy Wilson

Production management:
Susan McCallister, Sarah Wallis

Field-testing and networking:
Amina La Cour Mini, Nicole Perez, Tawnia
Queen, Rebecca Ratcliff, Kathryn Young

Additional illustrations:
Sara Boore, Barbara Carter, Joy Conway,
Christine Eber, Regina Faul-Doyle, Sandy
Frank, Anna Kallis, Susan Klein, Joyce
Knezevich, Gabriella Nuñez, Kate Peatman,
Nicole Perez, Petra Röhr-Rouendaal, Mona
Sfeir, Christine Sienkiewicz, Sarah Wallis,
Lihua Wang, David Werner

Copy editing:
Todd Jailer, Jane Maxwell

Proofreading:
Leona Benten

Editorial oversight:
Sarah Shannon, Todd Jailer

*And all the other staff and volunteers at Hesperian
whose efforts made this book possible.*

Thanks

A special thanks to all the funders of this book and the Early Assistance Series:

This publication was made possible
through support provided by
Plan International, Childreach —
the US member of Plan International,
DANIDA — Royal Danish Ministry of

Foreign Affairs, The May and Stanley Smith Charitable Trust, United Nations
Children's Fund (UNICEF), and the US Agency for International Development
(under the terms of Cooperative Agreement No. 442-A-00-02-00172-00). The
opinions expressed herein are those of the authors and do not necessarily reflect
the views of the US Agency for International Development nor those of our other
committed supporters.

Some of these supporters have also been collaborators, sharing their understanding
of the needs of parents and health promoters working with children. They have
reviewed and field-tested early versions of this book, improving it immeasurably.

Advisors and reviewers

How to help children who are deaf communicate is a very controversial topic. We are especially grateful to the many committed people who gave so freely of their guidance and opinions despite the inclusion of ideas they may not have completely agreed with.

This book could not have been written without the help of parents, teachers, deaf adults, and health workers from around the world, who shared their experiences, stories of the challenges they faced, and solutions they found.

Thanks to the following groups who contributed so much of their hearts and minds in reviewing draft materials:

in Bangladesh:
Center for Disability in Development

in Cameroon:
Abundant Life Ministry for Blind and Deaf Children

in People's Republic of China:
Tianjin Hearing Disability Rehabilitation Center

in Ghana:
Ashanti School for the Deaf

in Haiti:
Pazapa

in India:
Balavidyalaya

in Jamaica:
Clarendon Group for the Disabled, Jamaica Association for the Deaf

in Mongolia:
The School for Deaf and Blind Children

in Tanzania:
Chama Cha Viziwi Tanzania (CHAVITA)

in Uganda:
Uganda Society for Disabled Children

in Vietnam:
Catholic Relief Services, Pearl S. Buck International

in Zimbabwe:
NZEVE Deaf Children's Centre

Thanks also to Fundación Puntos de Encuentro for facilitating review of parts of Chapter 1 in Nicaragua with members of the Centro Fé, Esperanza y Amor, Escuela Cristiana de Sordos in Managua; Asociación por un Mundo sin Barreras in Chinandega; and the Asociación Nacional de Sordos de Nicaragua (ANSNIC).

Several stories in this book were adapted from articles written by the following persons or organizations:

Thanks to Judith Collins (page 103), Birgit Dyssegaard (pages 142, 161, and 166), Elina Lehtomaki (page 148), Asocicao de Pais e Amigos dos Surdos do Cabo (page 150), M. Miles (page 162), Paul Mumba (page 163), and EENET — Enabling Education Network and DICAG — Disabled Childrens Action Group (page 189).

The hearing aid checklist (page 226) is reproduced with the kind permission of Balavidyalaya, in India.

We also wish to express our thanks to the many advisors, reviewers, and others who shared their knowledge and expertise:

Carol-lee Aquiline, World Federation of the Deaf, Finland

Jonathan Brakarsh, Family Support Trust, Zimbabwe

Freda Briggs, Australia

Arlene Brown, Speech, Language, and Hearing Sciences, University of Colorado, USA

Gonzalo Delgado, Plan Internacional, UK

Charlie Dittmeier, Maryknoll Deaf Development Program, Cambodia

Birgit Dyssegaard, DANIDA, Denmark

Jill Ellis, Center for the Education of the Infant Deaf, USA

Roxanna Pastor Fasquelle, Mexico

Teresa Glass, USA

Gulbadan Habibi, UNICEF

Kathleen Huff, Catholic Relief Services, Vietnam

Khairul Islam, Plan International, Bangladesh,

Namita Jacob, Chetana, India

Patrick Kangwa, Inclusive Education, Zambia

Liisa Kauppinen, World Federation of the Deaf, Finland

Margaret Kennedy, Trainer on Disability & Abuse, UK

Elina Lehtomaki, University of Syvaskyla, Finland

Susie Miles, EENET, UK

David Morley, TALC, UK

Nancy Moser, Center on Deafness, UCSF, USA

Natalia Popova, Los Pipitos, Nicaragua

Shannon Reese, USA

Charles Reilly, Gallaudet University, USA

Rosalinda Ricasa, Gallaudet University, USA

Marilyn Sass-Lehrer, Gallaudet University, USA

Judy Shepard-Kegl and James Shepard-Kegl, Nicaraguan Sign Language Projects, Inc., USA

Andrew Smith, World Health Organization

Theresa Smith, American Sign Language and Interpreting School of Seattle, USA

Ester Tallah, Plan International, Cameroon

Abiola Tilley-Gyado, Plan International, UK

Andrew Tomkins, Institute for Child Health, UK

Joanne Travers, USA

Madan Vashista, USA

Susan Wecht, USA

Cindy Weill, Catholic Relief Services, Vietnam

Amy Wilson, Gallaudet University, USA

Sheila Wirz, UK

Doreen Woodford, Deaf Africa Fund, UK

Gabriela Woodman, Jean Weingarten Peninsula Oral School for the Deaf, USA

Owen Wrigley, Burma

Medical reviewers
Brian Linde, USA
Chris Forshaw, Uganda
Mike C.F. Smith, UK and Nepal

Contents

About this book

In this book we offer information, explanations, suggestions, examples, and ideas to help you respond in a flexible and creative way to the needs of the whole child. Every child who is deaf or cannot hear well is unique and will be helped most by approaches and activities that are lovingly adapted to her specific abilities and needs.

As much as we can, we try to explain basic principles and give reasons for doing things. After understanding the basic principles behind different activities or exercises, parents can begin to make adaptations. They can make better use of local resources and of the opportunities that exist in their own area.

In this book, we define 'a child who is deaf' as a child who is unable to hear anything. We use 'a child who cannot hear well' to describe a child who has some hearing loss but can hear some sounds (many people call this 'hard of hearing'). Sometimes, when we refer to both groups together, we use both terms — 'children who are deaf or cannot hear well'. But sometimes, for simplicity's sake, we use one term or the other, meaning to include all children with hearing loss.

ABOUT THE PICTURES

Since this book is written for people around the world who care for children with hearing problems, the drawings show people from many places. We hope these drawings will remind you that people all over the world face the same challenges you do.

HOW WE SHOW COMMUNICATION IN THIS BOOK

We show communication in 3 different ways in this book: speaking, thinking, and signing (using the hands and body to communicate in sign language).

When people speak
we show it like this.

Adam, come here!

The rounded box that contains the words has a 'tail' that points to the speaker's head.

When people think
we show it like this.

I wonder where Adam went...

The 'cloud' that contains the words has circles that point to the person's head.

When people sign
we show it like this.

Adam is in the kitchen.

The box that contains the words has a line that points to a person's hands.

THERE ARE MANY SIGN LANGUAGES

There are probably as many signed languages in the world as there are spoken languages. Signed languages are as old as history. They are not usually new languages recently invented. In many countries there is a national sign language for official use. Many countries also have regional sign languages.

Most of the pictures in this book show signs in American Sign Language because this book was written in the United States. (Some of the signs are in Mexican Sign Language or other national sign languages.) If you do not live in the United States, American Sign Language is **not** your sign language, and the deaf people in your community may not use or understand American Sign Language.

For example, although the spoken language in the United States, England, and Australia is the same, the sign language in each country is different. In the United States people use American Sign Language, in England people use British Sign Language, and in Australia people use Australian Sign Language.

In addition, many of the signs in our pictures are made-up signs, or are real signs but not the signs that match the words in the text. They are simply shown to give the idea of using sign language.

So please do not copy the signs in this book thinking you are learning sign language. If you do, the deaf people in your area may not understand you. Try to learn and use your own country's national sign language. Deaf people who sign are usually the best teachers.

ABOUT THE WAY WE USE 'HE' AND 'SHE' IN THIS BOOK

Most books about children who are deaf talk about the children as if they are all boys and use the word 'he' to refer to any child. This happens because society holds men to be more important than women and that belief is built into our language.

In fact, girls are not only left out of our language, they often receive less attention and care as well. This can include getting less food and getting less health care — both of which may contribute to deafness.

In a small way, we have tried to reflect a more equal world by using both 'he' and 'she' to refer to children. Because 'he or she' is awkward, we use 'he' in some sections and 'she' in others. If at times this is confusing, please pardon us.

Remember, **all** children need and deserve our love and support.

TO START USING THIS BOOK

The first chapter of this book explains the kinds of problems many children and families face when a child cannot hear well. Chapter 2 explains how parents and others can make a difference by helping children develop to the best of their ability. Chapter 2 also describes what you will find in the different parts of this book.

Within each chapter we point to other places in the book you might want to look for additional information.

Chapter 1
Hearing difficulties and communication

All over the world there are many children who are either deaf or can hear very little. Parents may never know what caused their child to be deaf. The deafness may be the result of an ear infection, an illness such as meningitis, an injury, or may be inherited. For information about causes of deafness see Chapter 15.

Like all children, children who are deaf or cannot hear well need love, attention, friendship, a sense of belonging, and an education. Because they do not hear, these children cannot learn language without help, and without language they cannot communicate with others, express themselves, or learn as easily as other children.

But with early help, children who are deaf can learn a language just like any child. So the most important resources for children who are deaf are parents, family members, and friends who take the time to help them learn to communicate.

With support, families of children with different hearing abilities can create homes and communities where their children are accepted and their strengths recognized — where they can make friends, learn, and lead happy lives.

Why communication is important

A child learns language very quickly in the first years of life. It is important that a child's hearing problem be recognized early and that he receives effective help. If not, the best years for learning communication skills may be lost (birth to age 7). The earlier a child begins to learn a language and to practice communicating, the more he can learn.

> **Communication** happens when we **understand** what is being said to us and **respond**, and when we **express** our thoughts, needs, and feelings so they can be understood.

THE LONELINESS OF A DEAF CHILD

For a child, being deaf can be like living with a glass wall around him. A child who is deaf can see people talking but he cannot understand what they are saying.

People can interact with each other because they have learned a language to communicate with. But a deaf child cannot learn a language that he does not hear. This means many deaf children grow up not being able to learn or use a language to interact with others around them.

People have a strong need to communicate with each other and to build relationships. When a child does not have the communication skills to relate to other people, and when other people do not know how to communicate or relate with him, he may be left alone most of the time, even by the people closest to him. After a while he becomes socially isolated.

My neighbors don't like to look after Akhila when I have to go to the market. They say she doesn't understand anything they say.

Sometimes other children come running behind us and call Habib bad names. I wish I could protect him from all this meanness.

COMMUNICATION FOR LEARNING AND THINKING

Children use communication to learn about the world, to relate to other people, to express themselves, and to think and develop their ideas. Without some form of communication, a deaf child cannot fully develop her mind or abilities.

The more children are able to learn a language, the more they can understand their world, think and plan, and develop close relationships with the people around them.

For more information about language and children's development, see Chapter 2.

Hi. My name is Carmen and I use my hands to communicate because I am deaf. I went to a school for deaf children in Nicaragua. There, we made up Nicaragua's first sign language. I still remember what it was like to finally have people understand me.

It is as though I have colors to paint the whole world, where before I had only gray.

It is so exciting to FINALLY be able to EXPRESS myself

I CAN TELL MY FRIENDS about my plans and what my family is like and even about my grandmother's CHICKENS that ran in and out of our house....

I will tell you my story, but first I want to tell you the stories of some other children who cannot hear.

Not every child goes to a school like mine. Anita is deaf like me but she was not able to learn to communicate. Here is Anita's story.

Anita's story

Anita was born almost completely deaf, but her parents did not realize this until she was 4. When she was a baby, they only saw that she was healthy and energetic. Until her sister Lora was born, they didn't worry that Anita wasn't learning to talk. They thought she was just a little slow to develop.

"Are you sure she can hear?" a neighbor asked one day. "Oh yes," said Anita's mother, Eva. Eva called her name loudly and Anita turned her head.

But when she was 3, Anita could still only say a few words. Her 2-year-old sister Lora was saying new words every day. Lora smiled and laughed more than Anita when Eva talked or sang to her. So Eva talked and sang more to Lora than to Anita. Lora asked for things, sang simple songs, and played happily with other children. Anita played by herself, since playing with other children often ended in fighting or crying.

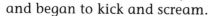

Once in the village market, Lora asked for a hair ribbon and Eva bought her one. A moment later Anita quietly picked up another ribbon and began to put it in her hair. Embarrassed and upset, Eva took it away. Anita threw herself on the ground and began to kick and scream.

When Anita's father heard what had happened in the market, he looked angrily at Anita and said, "When will you learn to ask for things? You're 4 years old and still don't even try to talk. Are you stupid or just lazy?"

Anita looked at her father. She could not understand what her father said. But she understood the angry look on his face. Tears rolled down her cheeks. Her father softened and took her in his arms.

When the family sat down that evening to talk, Eva remembered her neighbor's question about Anita's hearing. She decided to try making different sounds behind Anita's back to see what she could hear. When the family saw that Anita did not respond to most of the sounds, they realized she was deaf. It was a very sad day for them all.

Anita's family worried that Anita would never be able to develop like other children.

How can I explain things to someone who does not hear or speak? I want her to have a normal life like her sister. What kind of future can a deaf girl have?

Anita's parents did their best to help her. They were very busy taking care of their other children and their fields, so it was hard for them to give Anita the attention she needed. They hoped that someday Anita could have a full life, but they did not know how they could help her.

Anita is not stupid. Because no one ever taught her language and learned how to communicate with her, Anita and those around her frequently misunderstood and disappointed each other.

Anita and other deaf children may behave badly because they do not understand what they should do. Because Anita cannot hear words clearly, it is much more difficult for her to learn her family's language. So she has trouble understanding what people want and telling them what she wants.

It is no surprise that children who cannot hear well sometimes feel lonely or forgotten, develop 'behavior problems', or are slow in learning to relate to other people. Anita needs help to develop language so she can understand the world around her.

This is Omar's story. Omar was not born deaf. He lost his hearing after he learned to talk.

Omar's story

Omar was born with normal hearing and was a very talkative boy. For a couple of years he had many ear infections. His family could not afford to buy medicine to treat them. With each infection he lost a little more hearing. By the time he was 4 he could not understand his parents when they talked to him. He just looked at them in a puzzled way, and spoke less and less.

I think Omar can still hear some sounds.

Omar's grandfather, who had lost much of his hearing in his old age, suggested some things that might help. He said he usually understood people fairly well by using what hearing he still had and by watching people's lips.

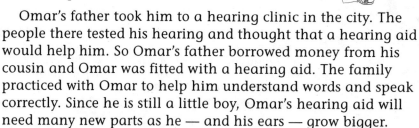

But, Omar's grandfather said, it was sometimes difficult to understand people because so many words look alike on the lips. He wondered whether a hearing aid would help Omar.

Omar's father took him to a hearing clinic in the city. The people there tested his hearing and thought that a hearing aid would help him. So Omar's father borrowed money from his cousin and Omar was fitted with a hearing aid. The family practiced with Omar to help him understand words and speak correctly. Since he is still a little boy, Omar's hearing aid will need many new parts as he — and his ears — grow bigger.

Some children like Omar, who can hear a little, may be able to speak and read lips. A hearing aid can help Omar because he has some hearing. It also helps that he understood language before he became deaf.

Omar's parents will probably have to struggle to find money for batteries and new parts for his hearing aid as he grows. If they are able to do this, Omar will do fine.

Here is Julia's story. When Julia's parents realized she was deaf, they made up signs to use with her.

Julia's story

Irene and Pedro realized their daughter Julia was deaf when other children her age were talking but she had not yet learned to speak.

Irene was determined that Julia would have every chance to learn and succeed in life. Despite her doubts, fears, and many questions, Irene thought, "Just because she can't hear doesn't mean she can't learn how to do things."

Irene remembered the time she met a foreign woman who spoke a different language. While they weren't able to talk to each other, they used gestures and acted out what they wanted to say. Even though it took more time and they sometimes misunderstood each other, they enjoyed themselves.

Julia is so smart. Look how quickly she learns new signs. And now Miguel is learning them too.

So to communicate with Julia, the whole family made up gestures and 'home signs' and used them together. Even the neighbors began to learn how to use Julia's home signs.

Then Irene asked a teacher at the village school when Julia could start. The teacher said that she did not have any way to teach deaf children. She told Irene about a school that might be able to teach Julia, but it was a 2-hour walk there and back. Pedro and Irene wondered how old Julia would have to be before she could go there by herself every day.

The human desire to communicate is very strong. When parents learn how to communicate with gestures and home signs, little girls like Julia can blossom into smart, happy children.

But every child has the right to an education! How can Julia continue to learn? It was only because of how things changed in my country that I was able to go to school.

Before I tell my own story, you must first know about Nicaragua, the country in Central America where I live, and how it was when I was growing up.

Education for disabled children in Nicaragua

For many years Nicaragua was ruled by the Somoza family. They controlled most of the country's wealth and provided the people with few services.

The Somozas did not consider education important for everyone. They felt that people who spent their lives working in the fields did not need to go to school. Somoza himself said, "I don't want educated people, I want oxen!"

As a result, most people in Nicaragua could not read or write. Many children — the poor, the disabled, almost all children in rural areas, and especially children who were deaf — could not go to school.

People with power find it easy to treat those who are different from themselves as though they have fewer rights and are less than human.

This happens to poor people, people who speak a different language, women, those who practice a different religion and especially to people with a disability!

Then in 1979 the Nicaraguan people overthrew the Somoza dictatorship and brought in a new government. The new government believed everyone had a right to be educated and made education available to all children, including those who were deaf. For the first time in Nicaragua, a school for deaf children was opened.

EDUCATION IS A RIGHT FOR ALL CHILDREN

When everyone is committed to education, deaf children can have the chance to learn, go to school, and develop their capabilities just like everyone else!

Carmen's story

Some months after I was born, an illness spread quickly through many children in my village. I got sick too, with a very high fever. My parents were thankful when I got better, but they realized that the illness had left me deaf. As I grew older, we all felt frustrated because it was so hard to communicate even simple ideas or needs. My family did not know how to communicate with me or how to teach me.

> If I wanted something, I had to show my family by pointing at it. If it was not there to point at, I could not make them understand.

After the revolution in Nicaragua, a school for deaf children opened and my parents took me there. They realized the school could help me in ways they could not. The teachers at the school tried to teach us all to read lips and to speak. Even though many of us could not learn to read lips and speak well, just being together began to open up the world for us.

> I had never known another deaf child. Most of my new classmates had never met other deaf children either. When I saw the other children use signs, I began to use them too. For the first time, I began to learn.

Many of us started school as older children. We communicated using 'home signs' we had used with our families, and which were all different. But we taught each other these signs and made up new signs together. It was easy for us to use signs to communicate. As we used more and more signs, it grew into a real language. Soon we were able to communicate many things to each other, about our families and friends, our plans and dreams, and things that happened to us.

LANGUAGE MAKES LEARNING AND COMMUNITY POSSIBLE

Carmen and the other deaf young people in Nicaragua proved to the world that sign language is a natural and complete language that develops in a community. As with any other language, to use sign language you need a group of people to use it with.

As Carmen and other children developed the Nicaraguan sign language and their communication skills, they also developed abilities to describe things, solve problems, and make their feelings, needs, and ideas known. Sign language not only gave the children a way to communicate, it helped them develop their ability to think.

Sign language lets me speak with others, learn about the world, and say what I think. I am no longer alone, feeling frustrated, or confused. Sign language — my language — lets me be a part of a community.

Accepting differences can bring people together

Deaf people are different in the way they understand and use language to communicate and express themselves. Rather than pretending that differences do not exist, it is wiser to accept the differences *Do not turn away — I am not ashamed. I am proud to be deaf!* and use them to bring people together. Many hearing people say that deaf people have helped them become 'warmer' and more expressive in how they relate to others.

One of the reasons the Nicaraguan children developed such a complete language is there were many children using it. They could do this because the people of Nicaragua decided to put more of their resources into education. They started an educational reform movement that created a strong school system for all children — including children who were deaf or could not hear well.

Coming together for deaf rights

Thanks to the Nicaraguan people's struggle to make education available to all, hundreds of young deaf people were brought together in schools for the first time. In one generation, the children began to produce a new and different form of communication — which developed into Nicaraguan Sign Language.

By the mid-1980s, these young deaf adults began meeting and working to promote their rights as deaf people. They formed the National Association of the Deaf of Nicaragua (ANSNIC). The people of ANSNIC helped to develop and promote Nicaraguan Sign Language, publishing a dictionary as well as a book for children. They worked with the Ministry of Education to begin to include signing in the deaf schools, and to improve the programs for deaf education.

Today, ANSNIC is a powerful group in Nicaragua that works for the rights of deaf people and also serves as a social center for its members.

All children can learn to communicate

Children who have different hearing abilities can communicate with gestures, home signs, a complete sign language, and lip-reading and speaking. Some children who can hear a little will be able to speak and read lips. Other children communicate best by making signs with their hands. Young deaf children can learn sign language easily and naturally — just like young hearing children learn a spoken language.

To feel good about themselves and to have a sense of belonging, it is important for deaf children to meet each other and also to meet adults who are deaf.

There may be a deaf person in the community who can teach children sign language.

Some families are able to send their child to a special school for deaf children. Other families teach their children at home. Some children may be helped by getting a hearing aid from a clinic and learning to read lips.

Whatever type of communication you use, this book will try to help you communicate with your child.

Every family has its own story about the difficulties they faced and what they did to help their child. Sharing these stories can help families find ways to help their children learn and feel secure.

Chapter 2
Children who cannot hear well need help early

In their first years of life, all children, including children who are deaf or cannot hear well, will learn more skills and learn them more quickly and easily than at any other time in their lives. Their physical development is easy to see. First they crawl, and then they walk and run.

Now it's your turn!

Children also start to develop mentally as soon as they are born. The baby's brain is like a sponge that has a great capacity to absorb and learn new things. During the first years, children who can hear learn language very quickly. As their language and communication develop, their ability to think also grows. That is why it is very important for parents to help children who are deaf or cannot hear well learn a language as early as possible. With a language, children who cannot hear well can also develop their mental abilities.

Papa, where does the sun go at night?

To sleep?

What do you think, Hari?

How children develop new skills

Every child develops in 4 main areas: body (physical), thinking (mental), talking and listening (communication), and getting along with other people (social). In each area, a child learns new skills step by step.

For example, before a child can learn to walk, she must first learn many simple kinds of body control:

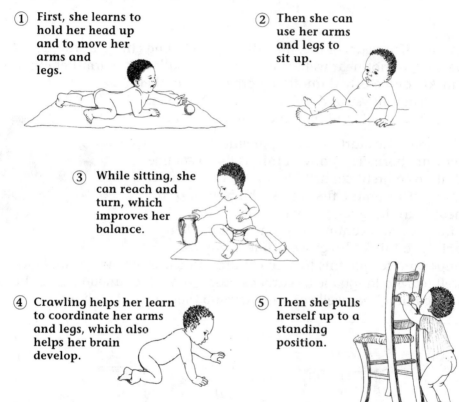

(1) First, she learns to hold her head up and to move her arms and legs.

(2) Then she can use her arms and legs to sit up.

(3) While sitting, she can reach and turn, which improves her balance.

(4) Crawling helps her learn to coordinate her arms and legs, which also helps her brain develop.

(5) Then she pulls herself up to a standing position.

In all areas of development, each new skill a child learns builds on the skills she already knows and makes it possible for her to learn other, more difficult skills.

When a child does not learn a skill, she cannot learn other skills that depend on it. For example, if she has a problem holding up her head, she will then have difficulty learning skills like sitting or crawling, in which holding up the head is important.

Each new skill builds on already-learned skills, like building blocks.

CHILDREN'S COMMUNICATION SKILLS AND LANGUAGE ALSO DEVELOP STEP BY STEP

Children's language develops in the same way as their physical skills. They learn simple skills first.

(1) Babies begin to express their thoughts, needs, and feelings by making sounds or using facial expressions and pointing.

(2) They hear and understand other people's words.

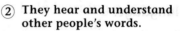

Where is mama?

Do you want some more?

(3) They begin to use words. They know and use names of the people closest to them.

(4) Later they start to talk and express themselves more completely.

Nana?

Yes, sweetheart?

Can I have some?

(5) Words help them think and learn new things.

That's right, Mari.

All clean!

Learning language

When you are surrounded by words, it is easy to learn the language that people in a community speak. Children learn language as they listen to people talk to each other and watch what happens, and as they talk to other people. Language becomes a way for them to understand their experiences and how the world around them works.

Deaf children need help early

With help, children who cannot hear can communicate and learn language. Since babies start learning as soon as they are born, it is important that families begin giving extra attention to communication to help their deaf children as soon as possible. If children who cannot hear well have help to learn a language — and that language may be a sign language — they can understand and communicate with people around them. Then they can learn what other children usually learn by hearing.

Do you want another kiss from mama?

What did Grandma ask us to buy?

Tea.

If the child's hearing problem is noticed early and effective help is provided, the best years for learning language and communication skills (birth to age 7) will not be lost. See Chapters 7, 8, and 9 for more information about helping a child learn language.

How to know if your child needs help

Babies develop at their own pace. Some develop more quickly than others. But most children grow and develop new skills at about the same age. By age 2, most children can speak or sign about 50 to 200 words. A child usually knows about 900 words at age 3, and 1500 words by age 4.

The important thing is that a child continue to learn new skills. But when a child is not learning a skill even long after other children her age have learned it, this is usually a sign that she may have a problem or need extra help.

This chart describes some of the communication skills children learn and when most children learn them. Parents can use the chart to decide which skills their children already know, and which skills they need to learn. To decide what activities to do first, start by asking yourself, "Is my child doing everything that other children his age are doing?" For more information on the ages and order in which children usually learn new skills, see the Child Development Charts on pages 231 to 238.

3 months

- responds to familiar voices or faces
- reacts to sudden sounds or movements

6 months

- makes simple sounds or gestures
- turns head toward movements or sounds

1 year

- joins sounds together or repeats hand shapes
- begins to name things
- understands and responds to simple words or signs
- imitates single signs

ba-ba ga-ga

2 years

My cup.

- uses simple words or signs
- uses sentences with 2 and 3 words or signs
- knows 50 to 200 words or signs

3 years

- understands most simple language
- knows and uses 500 to 1000 words or signs

Where is the biscuit?

I ate it.

5 years

- talks or signs about what he has done
- asks many questions

What are those people doing?

NOTE: Some children who cannot hear well may have other problems. Their minds and bodies could be slow to develop for other reasons. See the book ***Disabled Village Children*** for more information on how to help a child whose mind and/or body are slow to develop.

YOU CAN HELP YOUR CHILD LEARN

If you think your child's communication is not developing as it should, you can help him learn. Parents often think that only someone with professional training can help their child. But as a parent, you know your child better than anyone else, so you can make a big difference in his development.

Other children Ali's age know how to behave with each other. I think it's important for him to learn how to get along with other children.

In Chapters 3 to 9 you can find information about:

- guidelines for teaching language (Chapter 3)

- basic communication skills (Chapter 4)

- finding out what your child can hear (Chapter 5)

- listening skills (Chapter 6)

- choosing and learning a language (Chapter 7)

- learning a sign language (Chapter 8)

- learning a spoken language (Chapter 9)

What's that sign?

'Fix'. Can you sign 'fix'?

Chapter 3
Guidelines for
teaching language

A child who is deaf or cannot hear well learns to communicate by seeing. He will not learn words like others do, just by listening to people talk. He needs a longer time and more help to learn a language — whether by watching and listening to people talk, or by seeing them sign. He may start earlier than other children to pay attention to written words. When he sees written words, such as his own name, he can make the connection between a word and its meaning.

The guidelines in this chapter can make it easier for parents and others to teach children how to use a language. Try using these guidelines while working on the activities in this book.

Communicate as much as you can

Helping deaf children learn a language is the most important thing that parents and others can do. Even if people generally do not talk to children as they do their work, your child needs everyone to make extra efforts to speak to her. Communication is the only way she will learn.

Sometimes parents may feel ashamed of a child who cannot hear well. Or the child may be protected too much. But a child needs to take part in her family's activities. Being left alone will stop her from learning many things.

Throughout the day, look for opportunities to communicate with your child. Include her in activities with other people, so she gets used to seeing and hearing different people communicate. Encourage the whole family — brothers, sisters, grandparents, and other relatives — to do this too.

Are you coming to the market today?

Yes. Ashaki and I will bring some cassava and mangoes.

A child needs to take part in her family's activities.

Fitting activities into your family's daily life

It is important to think about how to support your child's development in ways that make sense for your family. Some of the activities in this book will take extra time to do or may change the way you usually do things.

Your child will learn better when teaching becomes a part of everyday activities.

If we take good care of the bean plants, they will grow big and strong.

Big!

- Talk or sign to your child while you do activities together, like eating, bathing, changing clothes, and so on. These are good times to talk and sign because you are close to your child and he is usually paying attention to you.

Shirt.

Lihua's mother is using home signs to communicate.

To describe what you do, use the same signs or words for the same things, each time. This will help your child learn the meaning of signs and words, and help him to use signs and words (see Chapter 4, pages 37 to 46).

- As much as possible, keep your child nearby while you work. Make many short comments about what you are doing.

Are you hungry? Can you smell the rice? Mmm!

Cesar's mother is using sign language to communicate.

- Talk and sign about what you think your child is seeing, doing, and feeling, as if you were him.

Yuck! Don't like spinach...

Jawad's cousin is using words and expressions on the face to communicate.

- Follow the child's interests. Make activities using things your child is interested in.

A pineapple! What else do we need?

BE REALISTIC

- Try to be realistic about how much time you and others can spend working with your child.

- Try to adapt activities so they fit more easily into your daily life and take less time.

When I weave, I can talk about colors, and Teresa will learn the names of colors when she gives me the yarn.

- Try breaking large tasks into smaller, easier steps. This way you will see progress and not get discouraged.

I want Ravi to learn to say his name.

Why not start with each separate sound first — like 'Ra' and 'vi'?

Many people can help do these activities

Though children need the care and love of both their parents, parents do not have to be a child's only teachers. Let friends, neighbors, and other family members help. Get to know deaf people who use the local sign language. It is especially important for the child who is deaf or cannot hear well to have many people doing activities with him because:

- it will help him learn to communicate with many people including other deaf people.
- he will learn to get along with different people.
- other people will learn how to interact with deaf people.

I don't have much time to help Mira since my husband had to go away to work. I have to take care of our fields, as well as the house and the children.

My neighbor's eldest daughter is helping our son learn to speak every afternoon. Maybe she could teach Mira at the same time.

That's a good idea! We are also very busy, but we showed my mother-in-law ways to help our daughter.

Parents who have children that are deaf or do not hear well can work together to solve problems (see page 184).

Some people, sometimes even close family members, may not want to spend time with deaf children. Other people, even if they want to help, do not know how. You can help them learn about deafness and how being deaf makes it more difficult for someone to learn a language. They may become more comfortable if they know what to do.

Share what you have learned about hearing problems, the activities you and your child are working on, and the reasons for doing these activities.

TALK WITH YOUR FAMILY

Everyone in a family plays a role in a child's life. Each person caring for a child, especially one with special needs, may have different ideas about the best way to raise and help that child. It is important for all those who care for the child to find time to talk together and

Let me watch Thuy for the weekend so you can get some rest.

understand each others' ideas. And if one of you is feeling tired or discouraged, the others may be able to help.

ASK OTHERS FOR HELP

Parents can ask other community members and neighbors to help care for the deaf child.

When I was little, my parents used to take me to the market with them.

Mariama is explaining how her parents would bring her to the market...

Meet the deaf people in your community. Deaf adults remember what it felt like to be deaf children. They will probably be happy to help your family and your child.

Hearing people who use sign language can help you communicate with deaf adults if you do not know sign language.

Talk to a health worker or school teacher, or someone that teaches children who are deaf. This is especially helpful if your child does not seem to be learning new skills after several months.

I will write to Mrs. Patel. She is a deaf teacher in the city.

Children can help with these activities

Children can be very helpful. Usually brothers, sisters, and other friends of a deaf child learn sign language very quickly. As much as possible, let children take part in these activities.

Younger children can join the activities and older children can be teachers if you show them what to do. They can also teach a deaf child other skills and include him in their play. This will help him make friends and learn how to behave with others. This will also help the children who can hear learn about deafness and how to communicate with deaf children.

Older children are often natural teachers, and enjoy doing activities with younger children.

Suggestions for helping your child learn

LET YOUR CHILD TAKE THE LEAD

Children are most eager to learn when they are doing something they like. If your child seems interested in something, or likes to play with a special toy, make that an opportunity to help her communicate or learn.

Did you find a new game?

Let your child take the lead. It will keep her interested and help her learn that her decisions are important. She will know that she has some control over what happens. This is especially important for girls. In many places, girls are expected to be quiet and to follow instructions. Helping a girl make decisions and follow her own ideas can strengthen her confidence and abilities.

But just because you let your child take the lead does not mean you allow her to act badly or get into dangerous situations. Your guidance is important. And the knowledge you have about her language needs and abilities can help you guide her play so that she will learn.

MAKE COMMUNICATING FUN AND USEFUL

Children enjoy communicating when they have real things to sign or talk about, and people to sign or talk with. Try to give your child many opportunities to learn about the world and encourage her to sign and talk about what she is learning. Making conversation with your child will help her learn faster than if you ask her only to memorize and repeat signs and words.

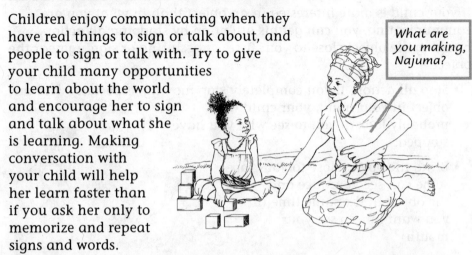

What are you making, Najuma?

LET YOUR CHILD HELP YOU DO WORK

As your child helps you do your work, communicate with him about what you are doing. Use words or signs to ask him to help you do something, to get you tools, or to help in other ways. Your child will be more interested in paying attention and communicating when he is helping you do something you both value.

GET YOUR CHILD'S ATTENTION BEFORE YOU COMMUNICATE

A child who cannot hear well needs to watch your lips move or see you gesture or sign to understand you. He also gets a lot of information from seeing the look on your face. So it is important to wait until he is looking at you before you begin to talk or sign.

Suren's brother touches his arm to get his attention.

To get a child's attention, move or wave your hand where he can see you, call his name, touch him, or hit a nearby object to make a loud noise so the child can feel the vibrations.

Other ways to get your child's attention

If your child is more interested in an object than in what you are communicating, you can get his attention by stopping all action, bringing the object close to your face, or gesturing or signing near the object.

- Stop all action. If you completely stop moving, especially with an object in your hand, your child will probably look at you to see why you have stopped.

- Bring the object close to your face, so he can see your face and the object at the same time (if you want him to see your mouth).

- Point to or sign near the object (if you want him to learn a sign for the object).

To call his attention to the sign, Obasi's sister is signing near his toy.

At first, it can be hard to remember to get your child's full attention before you begin to communicate. But it gets much easier with practice.

SIGN OR TALK FACE TO FACE, AT EYE LEVEL

Your child will be able to understand more of what you say or sign if you squat down close to her (within about 1 meter, or 3 feet), and look her in the eye as you speak or sign.

If possible, try to have light from the sun or a lamp shining on your face, not from behind you. When the light comes from behind you, your face and hands will be in a shadow and harder to see.

Mariana's mother is playing a clapping game with her.

Sweet orange, half a lime, give me a hug so you'll...

...be mine!

It will be easier for your child to understand spoken words if you talk naturally and in a clear voice. Do not shout. Shouting makes the words harder to understand. Speak in short, simple sentences so you do not confuse her. It will be easier for your child to see your lips move if you do not have anything in or in front of your mouth while you are speaking.

What do you have there?

If your child can hear a little

These suggestions may help her hear sounds a little better.

- Cupping a hand behind the ear can help more sound reach the ear.

- Speaking close to a child's ear can help her hear better. This makes sounds louder and lessens the amount of noise from the environment. Remember she also needs to see your face while you are talking to her.

Let's go give Mrs. Chifeve her gift.

USE GESTURES, TOUCH, AND EXPRESSIONS ON THE FACE

All people use body movements, touch, and expressions on the face to help people understand what they want to say. Children often use touch to communicate with each other. Children who cannot hear well find touch extremely useful. A touch will help communicate your care and concern in a way that nothing else can. Sometimes movements and looks can take the place of a word or sign. At other times they add information to words and signs.

Help your child by using your body and face to communicate as much as possible. First, try to notice how you already do this. Then look for ways to add to what you do.

Good girl!

Try to make sure that the messages you send with your body and face are the same as those you send with words and signs. If the messages of your face do not match your words, your child will be confused.

Maria's angry expression sends a different message than her kind words. This is confusing.

REDUCE BACKGROUND DISTRACTIONS AS MUCH AS POSSIBLE

Background distractions, such as other children playing near your child, can make activities more difficult or even impossible to do. You can help by finding a place with few distractions. Try to get rid of any noises that are not necessary. When a room is noisy, a child who cannot hear well finds it more difficult to understand what is being said.

This father is shutting off the radio before playing with his son.

CHANGE ACTIVITIES TO SUIT YOUR CHILD

The activities in this book can help your child learn to communicate. But they are just examples of activities that can help a child learn. Watch your child carefully to see what interests him and makes him want to communicate — and also watch for what upsets him and makes him want to stop. Then you can think of ways to adapt the activities in this book so they will work better for your child and fit more easily into your family's daily activities.

You can also adapt these activities so they fit with your child's abilities. For example:

- If a child can hear some speech sounds, help him learn simple words by giving them emphasis and repeating them. Then use the words often throughout the day.

*It is hot. Do you want some **water**? I want **water** too.*

- If a child cannot hear speech sounds well, teach everyone some signs to use with him. See Chapter 8 for information about teaching sign language.

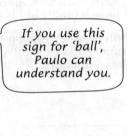

If you use this sign for 'ball', Paulo can understand you.

- If your child can hear some of the sounds around her, everyone can help her pay attention to sounds by pointing them out.

Did you hear? Someone is at the door.

Helping your child grow

If you make these activities part of your family's everyday life, your child will have a childhood that is full of fun and learning. As he grows up he can:

join in family conversations

develop friendships with other children

go to school and learn a trade

meet other children and adults who are deaf or cannot hear well

and years from now, marry and have a family of his own.

He will be able to support his family and be involved in the community.

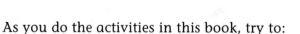

As you do the activities in this book, try to:

- be patient. Very young children can only pay attention for a few minutes at a time.

- be light-hearted. Learning activities will work only if they are fun for both of you.

Do not get discouraged. Do not expect immediate changes in a child's behavior. Your child will gain something from every activity, even if you do not notice it right away.

MAKE LEARNING FUN
~ Be patient
~ Be positive
~ Keep activities short

Chapter 4
Basic communication skills

People usually communicate by using words or signs. But children begin to communicate long before they learn these skills.

Communication happens when:

  • one person sends a message, and

  • another person receives the message and responds.

A young child sends a message by moving her body, making sounds, or changing the look on her face. When parents understand her movement and respond to her, they are already communicating.

This child is sending messages that:

She is excited.   **She wants her toy.**   **She is happy to see her mother.**

  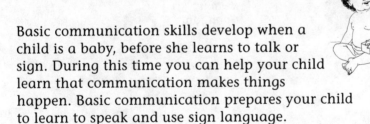

Mmm!

Aahh! Yes, Laila! Mama's back.

Basic communication skills develop when a child is a baby, before she learns to talk or sign. During this time you can help your child learn that communication makes things happen. Basic communication prepares your child to learn to speak and use sign language.

This chapter will help you understand how your baby can:

  • take turns.
  • pay attention to you.
  • understand you.
  • use gestures.
  • make sounds.

How children learn to communicate

Although a child communicates from birth, at first he does not realize he is doing so. He moves his body, makes sounds, or changes the look on his face because of the way he feels. For example, he might cry because he feels hungry or wet. Slowly, he sees that his messages make things happen. When he cries, someone comes to find out what is wrong. When he smiles, people smile back. So he begins to send messages to make things happen.

Communication is a powerful tool for getting what we want or need and understanding what other people want or need. You can help a child begin to communicate by responding to his movements, sounds, and looks on the face. This helps him learn that his actions have an effect on others.

Let your child take turns

Taking turns helps your child develop two-way communication skills. When he is older, this will help him learn how to make conversation with other people.

That's a ball.

Here, Kwame's mother Hola helps them get started.

Can I have the ball?

Hola's face shows she is asking a question.

Thank you, Kwame. Good job!

Your child will learn even more if you can keep a give-and-take going between you.

For example: Hola waits until Kwame is looking at her. She gets him interested and engaged by raising her eyebrows, smiling, and shaking the ball.

When Kwame is ready, Hola rolls the ball to him.

Kwame rolls the ball back to Hola. She smiles and claps her hands...

...and rolls the ball back to him.

Now Kwame knows what to do. He and his mother are taking turns.

Then Hola changes the game to keep Kwame's attention. She hides the ball inside a box. Notice Hola's face. How would your face look if you were asking, "Where is the ball?" without using words?

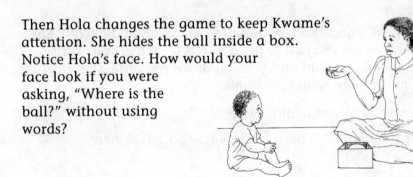

Hola waits while Kwame crawls to the box.

Hola smiles and claps her hands again when he finds the ball.

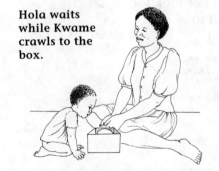

As you see in these pictures, basic communication begins when a child is very young. Communication does not have to include words.

To encourage your child to take turns

Every time you take turns with your child it will be different. Here are some general guidelines to make taking turns successful.

To begin:

- Get your child's attention and let her know you are ready to play.

> If your child does not respond in any way, try giving her a prompt, like a touch on her arm, to remind her it is her turn.

- Let your child take her turn first. You can then respond to what interests her. But if you have to wait a long time, go ahead and begin yourself.

> Wait until you have your child's attention before you take your next turn. Then try to take about the same amount of time for your turn as your child took for hers.

- Your child will know that you noticed her action and liked it. She will now try to use it again to get a response. When your child makes a sound or a sign and gets a positive response, she will want to make more sounds or signs.

When you respond to your child, try to:

- **copy** her sounds and actions (if she says "ga...ga," then you say "ga...ga").

- **continue** things that she likes (rolling the ball to her again).

- **add** to what she does (like making her look for the ball), to keep her attention and to help her learn new ways of playing.

> Allow your child to stop whenever she wants. At first, taking turns may last only a minute or two. But soon your child will want to take turns for a longer time.

As children grow, they will take turns more.

Older children who cannot hear also need to learn to keep a give-and-take going through whatever activities that interest them. For a child who is 5 years old, playing a game may be more interesting than rolling a ball.

Rene's older sister is teaching her a clapping game.

Preparing a child to use signs and to speak

While a child is learning that communication can make things happen, you can help her learn to understand words and signs. This will prepare her to use signs and to speak. To understand words and signs, she must first learn to pay attention to them and learn that words and signs have meanings. See Chapter 8 and Chapter 9 for suggestions to help your child learn the meaning of signs and words, and learn how to use signs and words herself.

ENCOURAGE YOUR CHILD TO USE HAND MOVEMENTS

It is natural for a child to use gestures. Both deaf and hearing people already use their hands, bodies, and make expressions with their faces to communicate many things — both with words and without words. These movements are called gestures. We wave 'good-bye', shake our heads when we mean 'no', and we point.

Here are some examples of people using gestures:

This child is telling his mother that he wants something.

Do you think it will rain?

This man is answering that he does not know.

Using gestures and signs does not prevent a child from learning to talk. **Gestures help prepare a child to sign and speak.** By using them he learns that he can send specific messages. For example, he learns that by shaking his head, he makes it clear he does not want to do something.

When you are with your child, expect him to use gestures, signs, or sounds. Your child needs to learn that his words or signs are important and that people react to his communication.

- Use gestures often to send messages to your child.

Sunil's aunt is using a gesture.

Titus' grandmother is using a gesture and word together.

No!

- Use the hand movements your child already uses to communicate. Many children begin to make up hand movements that name objects, people, or activities. If you watch for these movements, you and your family can begin to develop 'home signs'.

For example:

Tae Woo points at a bird.

Tae Woo makes a 'flying' movement to name the bird.

Tae Woo's mother uses his movement together with words.

A bird!

These signs are very useful for family members to communicate with each other but they may not be understood by other people. See page 40 for more information on home signs.

- Play games that help a child learn to point.

Where's mama?

Yes! Here's mama!

- Draw pictures of different family members, and of the foods your child usually eats, the objects he likes to play with, and the clothes he wears. Encourage him to point to what he needs.

- Help your child show what he feels by using gestures. He will remember the gestures you make and he will copy them.

COMMUNICATE WITH HOME SIGNS

When a family has a deaf child, gestures help them begin to communicate with each other. But people need more complete ways to communicate than simple gestures. Families often make up and use 'home signs', hand and body movements that they develop to express themselves and communicate with their deaf child.
Here is an example:

A Mexican man went to a village with his 6-year-old deaf son. When the boy wanted to go home, he pulled on his father's clothes. Then he used home signs that he and his family had made up.

Let's go (home)

riding the mule

please!

This boy is pulling on his father's clothes, pointing and also using home signs ('riding the mule' and 'please').

This helps him communicate more than he could by simply using gestures.

Making up and using home signs is natural for families with children who are deaf or cannot hear well. Other deaf and hearing people will probably not understand the signs you have made up, but you can share them with friends just as you have done with the family.

Your child and your family are probably using gestures and home signs right now. It makes sense to continue doing this. Even though home signs do not make up a complete language, they can be very helpful for expressing simple ideas and are a good start to communicating. To learn more about teaching your child the sign language that is used where you live, see Chapter 8.

Making up home signs

Making up signs can be fun. Remember, it will take time and patience. But there will be big rewards as you and your child begin to understand each other. The next few pages give ideas for making up signs. You can change them to fit the gestures, customs, and language of your area. You and your family will have many ideas for creating your own home signs.

Here are some suggestions to help you get started:

1. Try to make signs look like the things or actions you want to communicate:

baby

This sign for 'baby' looks like someone holding a baby.

2. Watch for signs your child makes up and use them. Many children, for example, make up signs to name people in the family.

Maria

One child made this sign for her sister, Maria, who wears glasses.

3. Use hand shape, position, and movement to make different signs. For example, when making the sign for drinking from a cup you could...

Shape your hand like a cup. Then move your hand as if you were drinking from the cup.

Or, if you wanted to sign about drinking from your hands, you could change your hand shape like this:

drink (from a cup)

drink (from hands)

4. Try to create similar signs for actions or things that go together. For example:

stand   lie down   jump

You can also create similar signs for opposites, like 'push' and 'pull'.

5. Combine signs for objects, actions, and ideas to create sentences. A child who learns to put ideas together will develop more complete communication skills.

"Put the cup on the table."

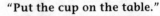

cup   cup on table

Examples of signs

These signs are from American Sign Language. You may find useful ideas for creating your own home signs from these signs, together with signs from your local sign language. These examples also show the many types of signs a child needs to know in order to communicate.

Signs for people

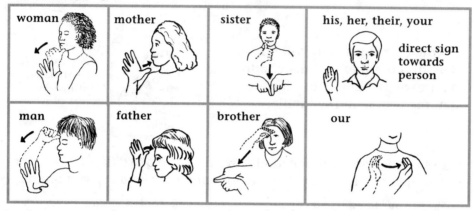

Signs for things

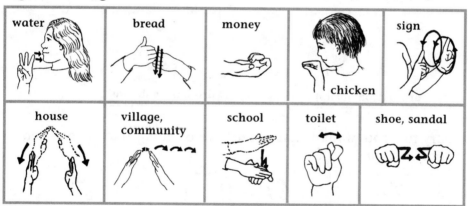

Describing signs

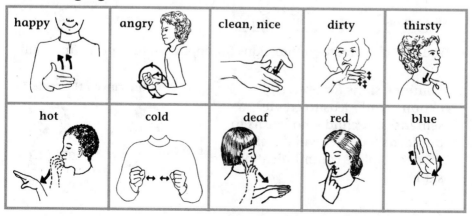

These examples also show how each sign can be changed and combined with other signs to give it new meaning.

Action signs

about doing something		about thinking		about relating to others	
start	stop	understand	forget	like	love
use	walk	want	don't want	help	play

Question signs

what	where	why	who	no	yes

Signs about direction

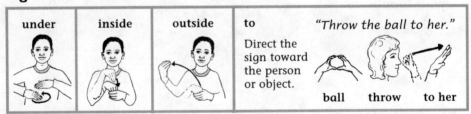

under	inside	outside	to	"Throw the ball to her."

Direct the sign toward the person or object.

ball   throw   to her

Signs about time

future	"It is going to rain."	past	"It rained."

future-sign   rain

past-sign   rain

now	"It is raining."	day	night

rain   now

ENCOURAGE YOUR CHILD TO MAKE SOUNDS

Children start using hand movements and gestures at an early age, and these can become the basis for developing communication and sign language. Children also start making sounds and noises at an early age, and these too can become the basis of communication and the development of spoken language.

Your child needs to learn that a person makes sounds with the lips, the tongue, the breath, and vibrations in the throat and nose.

Teach a child how sounds feel in his body, how to control his breath, and how to shape his mouth and tongue to make different sounds.

As you do the activities below, encourage your child to imitate you. It can be difficult for a deaf child to learn to make sounds. So when he does, let him know he has done something important.

- Lay your child on your chest. At first, let him feel your chest rise and fall as you breathe normally, without talking.

  Then talk or sing, letting your child feel the different ways your chest moves.

  La la la...

  Encourage him to feel the breath coming out of your mouth, too.

- In a natural voice, speak very closely (about 8 centimeters or 3 inches) to your child's ear. Speaking this close makes sounds easier to hear. Your child will also feel your breath as you speak.

  Manuel, what are you making with your blocks?

• Make up sounds that are easy to see on your lips and repeat them often during the day.

• Try matching a sound with an object.

Praise your child when he makes a sound or says a word.

• Try matching the length of a sign to a movement...   ...or the length of a word to a movement.

Encourage your child to make sounds by praising her as soon as she makes a sound or says a word. Small praise is enough — you can use a smile as praise. Or point to your ear and say, "I heard you." Or nod or say, "Yes." Remember, it is very difficult for her to learn how to speak clearly and to communicate using spoken words.

Wa?

Yes, Emilia! You want some water?

Here are 3 ways to show your child you are paying attention to his sounds:

- You can imitate him, showing that you enjoy imitating him. For example, if your child says "ooo" then you do that too, and wait to see if he does it again.

- You can respond to his sound like it is the beginning of a conversation. Try to understand what your child is communicating and answer it.

Aaaa?

Bird. That's a **bird** in the tree.

- You can ask him questions about what he is communicating. It will encourage him to start a conversation. Besides, asking questions is a good way to encourage him to ask you questions.

When your child has developed basic communication skills, he is ready to learn a language. For more information on learning a language, see Chapter 7. See Chapter 8 for information on learning sign language, and see Chapter 9 for information on learning a spoken language.

Chapter 5
What can your child hear?

Some children are completely deaf and cannot hear at all or can hear only very loud sounds. When babies are very young, parents notice their babies cannot hear, because they do not turn their head or respond, even to loud sounds.

Many more children with some hearing loss can still hear a few sounds. This sort of hearing loss can be harder for parents to notice. A child may show surprise or turn her head to a loud noise, but not to softer noises. She may respond only to certain kinds of sounds. Some children can still hear a little when people speak to them. They may slowly learn to recognize and respond to some words. But they do not hear all words clearly enough to understand. Children with this sort of hearing loss are slow to learn to speak.

Many children develop hearing loss because of repeated and long-lasting ear infections, or as a side effect of certain medicines (for causes of deafness see Chapter 18). Parents may not notice a child is slowly losing his hearing until he is maybe 4 or 5 years old and has not yet started talking, or is not talking clearly.

If you can find out early how much your child can hear, it will help you know what kind of extra help to give him so he can communicate. Sometimes parents, other children, or teachers think a child with hearing loss is mentally slow. If children who are deaf get extra help to learn to communicate, most of them can learn and be educated like other children. That is why it is important to find out what, if anything, a child can hear.

Understanding sound

If parents know about the different types of sounds, it will help them understand how much and what kind of sounds their children can hear.

LOUDNESS

Some sounds are louder than others. Noises that are closer are louder than the same noises farther away.

A motorcycle is much louder than a person walking. When a motorcycle is close by, it will sound much louder than a motorcycle farther away.

Some sounds can be made louder or quieter. For example, you can increase the loudness of a radio or you can make your voice quieter by changing from a shout to a whisper.

loud sound

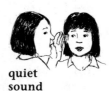
quiet sound

PITCH

Pitch is how high or low the tone of a sound is. Like in music, sounds can go up and down from high to low pitch.

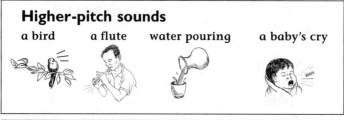

Higher-pitch sounds

a bird   a flute   water pouring   a baby's cry

Higher-pitch sounds have a sharp, thin sound that can feel like it goes right through your ears.

Lower-pitch sounds

a cow   a drum   thunder   a man's voice

Lower-pitch sounds have a full, heavy sound that you can feel in your bones.

Different speech sounds also have higher or lower pitches. For example, the sounds 'o-o-o' and 'm-m-m' have a low pitch. The sound 'e-e-e' has a medium pitch. The sounds 's-s-s' and 'f-f-f' have a high pitch.

There are many kinds of hearing loss

A child who has problems hearing usually has difficulty with both loudness and pitch. For example:

This baby does not hear well. She cannot hear **high-pitch sounds**.

She cannot hear her father playing the flute. But she can hear low-pitch, loud sounds like drums.

This boy cannot hear well. He cannot hear **low-pitch sounds**.

He cannot hear his father playing the drum, though he may feel its vibration (shaking). But he can hear high-pitch sounds like a baby crying.

This girl cannot hear well. She cannot hear **middle-pitch sounds**.

She can hear high-pitch sounds, so she can hear the baby crying. She can also hear low-pitch sounds like her father's voice. But she cannot hear her mother's voice.

This boy is completely deaf. He cannot hear **any sounds**.

He cannot hear his mother, the chickens in the yard, or the truck on the road, no matter how loud they are.

What sounds can your child hear?

If your child can hear a little, finding out which sounds she can hear will help you. The more you know about your child's hearing, the better you can communicate in a way she can understand.

NOTICE HOW YOUR CHILD RESPONDS TO SOUND

It can be difficult to know if and when a child hears a sound, especially with very young children. You will know if your child hears a sound because she may:

Ba!

- move her arms and legs.
- change the look on her face.
- become very still.
- make a sound herself.
- smile or laugh.
- turn toward the sound, or tilt her head to listen.
- be startled, open her eyes wider, or blink.

Does your child seem to hear some sounds?

To find out more about what a child can hear, watch him closely throughout the day and ask yourself:

- Does he seem to hear mostly high-pitch sounds? Or mostly low-pitch sounds? Or a mixture of both?
- Does he hear a sound some of the time but not all the time?
- Can he only hear sounds when the room is quiet?
- Does the sound have to be very loud for him to hear it?

When the room is quiet, Kofi can hear the blocks fall down.

Kofi may not hear the blocks fall down when there is other noise in the room.

CHECKING A CHILD'S HEARING AT HOME

It is hard to check a small child's hearing. But even if you plan to have your child's hearing tested by a professional, it is helpful if you can first check your child's hearing yourself. Then you can give information to

the professional and you can better understand what the professional is doing.

Also, checking hearing at home is free and uses materials that are easy to find. And doing the checking yourself will give you more confidence to decide about your child's care and development. It is also a good way for friends and family members to get more involved as your child learns to communicate.

Keep in mind that your child may respond to:

- what she sees, not to the sound.
- the vibration (shaking) that a loud sound makes.
- the expression on your face, or to your gesture.

And your child may not respond if:

- she is busy doing something.
- she is sick or has an ear infection.
- she is tired, bored, or in a bad mood.

How to check your child's hearing

Try to notice the sounds your child responds to in everyday settings. This is a good, general way to learn about your child's hearing. Next, you can check to see what kinds of sounds your child may or may not hear. You can first check to see what sounds she hears that different objects make, and then what 'speech' sounds she hears when people talk.

To do this, you need:

- a quiet place without other sounds or noise.
- some simple equipment.
- 2 people to help you.

First try to check the hearing of a child who is the same age as your child and whose hearing is normal. Practice until you see how a young child responds to hearing a sound.

- Keep the checking relaxed and enjoyable.

- Use a variety of small toys to keep the child from getting bored.

- Keep the sessions short. You can check hearing in more than one session.

▶ *Check for loudness and pitch of sounds*

One **helper** sits in front of a parent and child. He will get the child's attention by showing her a small toy.

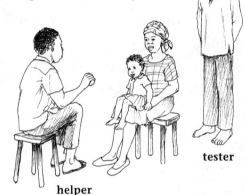

The other person stays 1 meter (3 feet) behind the parent, out of sight of the child. This person is the **tester.** He will make the sounds to each side of the child, for the child to hear. If the child turns to look at the tester, the tester should not interact with the child by smiling or looking at her.

tester

helper

What you will need to check hearing

In this test you will use simple sound makers made from 3 identical empty tin cans.

1. Put a piece of wood in the first tin can (low-pitch sound)

2. Put a handful of large uncooked dry beans in the second tin can (middle-pitch sound)

3. Put a handful of uncooked rice in the third tin can (high-pitch sound)

Shake the can gently for a **quiet** sound. Shake it harder for a **medium** sound. Shake it very hard for a **loud** sound. The tester should practice shaking each of the cans until he can control the loudness.

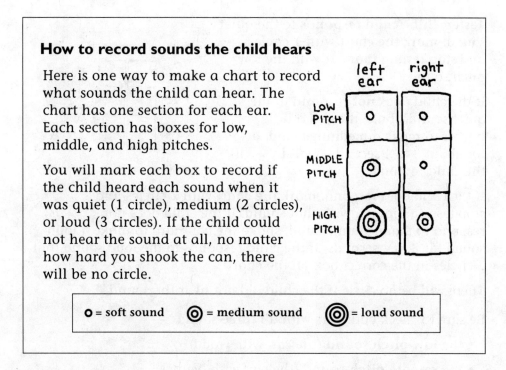

How to record sounds the child hears

Here is one way to make a chart to record what sounds the child can hear. The chart has one section for each ear. Each section has boxes for low, middle, and high pitches.

You will mark each box to record if the child heard each sound when it was quiet (1 circle), medium (2 circles), or loud (3 circles). If the child could not hear the sound at all, no matter how hard you shook the can, there will be no circle.

o = soft sound   ⊚ = medium sound   ◎ = loud sound

Testing the child

Helper: Calmly get the child's attention with the toy. When the child is paying attention to the toy, gently cover the toy with your other hand.

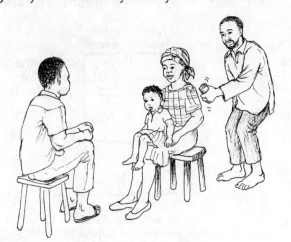

Tester: Use the can to make the low-pitch sound. Cover the top of the tin can and shake it for about 3 to 4 seconds behind **each** of the child's ears. First make a quiet sound.

Helper and parent: Notice if the child responds to the sound.

Helper: If the child responds, nod your head slightly to show the tester that the child responded.

Tester: If the child **responds** to the quiet sound, mark the chart with 1 circle and stop testing that ear with the low-pitch sound.

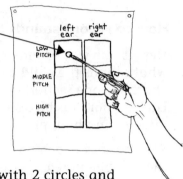

If the child **does not respond** to the quiet sound, shake the can a little harder to make a medium sound, also for about 3 to 4 seconds. Wait to see if the child responds.

If the child does respond, mark the chart with 2 circles and stop testing that ear with that sound. If the child does not respond to the medium sound, shake the can hard to make a loud sound for 3 to 4 seconds. If the child responds to the loud sound, put 3 circles in the correct box on the chart.

There will be no circle if the child did not hear the sound.

Be sure to check both ears with all three sounds —

- the **low-pitch sound** (the can with wood)
- the **middle-pitch sound** (the can with beans)
- the **high-pitch sound** (the can with rice)

When you have finished

Look at the pattern of hearing. It may be very different for each child.

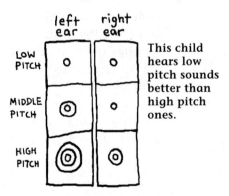

This child hears low pitch sounds better than high pitch ones.

The high pitch sounds have to be louder for her to hear them. She also hears better on her right side than on her left.

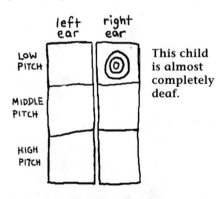

This child is almost completely deaf.

He can hear no sounds in his left ear. He can hear a little in his right ear, but only low pitch sounds that are loud.

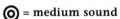 o = soft sound   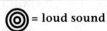 ◎ = medium sound   ◎ = loud sound

To get the best results

The **parent** should

- hold the child steady on her lap, but freely enough that the child can turn around.

- **not** react to any of the sounds made by the tester.

The **tester** should

- stay behind the child.

- make the sounds at the same height as the child's ears.

- make the sounds 1 meter (3 feet) from the child.

- **not** let the child **see** him, or his shadow or reflection.

- make the sounds on the **left** and **right** side of the child.

The **helper** should

- keep the child's attention on the toy.

- be calm and quiet.

- **not** look at the tester.

- **not** react to any of the sounds made by the tester.

CAN THE CHILD HEAR SPEECH SOUNDS?

Speech sounds also have differences in pitch. The speech sounds 't', 'd', 's', and 'sh', for example, have a higher pitch than sounds like 'oo', 'ee', and 'm'. This means your child may be able to hear some speech sounds but not others.

It will help to know if your child can hear high, middle, or low-pitch speech sounds, and how loud the sounds have to be for him to hear them. Try to notice the sounds he seems to hear when family members speak.

Children may seem to understand words when it is really the situation that makes the meaning clear. If someone says "Get the ball," while pointing or looking at it, the child may go to get the ball. He may not have heard the word but may have seen the person pointing at the ball.

To find out if he is hearing words or not, use 3 or 4 familiar objects in a game or as part of a daily task he already knows. Do this several times to find out if your child hears the names for the objects.

First, say the words without giving any clues.

Then, if your child did not understand the words alone, say the words, then look at the object.

Your child may also seem to hear sounds some times but not always. This does not mean your child is being stubborn. He just does not hear you. Many things can affect how he responds to sounds — like the time of day, hunger, or how your child is feeling that day. Colds and ear infections can also affect children's hearing temporarily.

If your child still does not understand, say the words, then look and point to the object.

▶ Check for speech sounds a baby or child can hear

In a speech test, instead of shaking a can to make a sound, the tester makes the sounds using his voice.

In this test you will use simple sounds.

1. The sound 'm-m-m-m-m' (humming) (low-pitch sound).

2. The sound 'oo-oo-oo-oo' ('oo' as in 'boot') (middle-pitch sound).

3. The sound 's-s-s-s-s' (hissing) (high-pitch sound).

The soft sound should be as quiet as possible. Ask a person with normal hearing to listen to you and tell you if she can hear the sound when you say it softly.

Sssssss.

The test is done in the same way as the loudness and pitch test. You start with the lowest pitch 'm-m-m-m', making the sound softly for 3 to 4 seconds behind the child's left ear. Continue in the same way — softer to louder, left ear then right ear, lower pitch to higher pitch. Be careful not to increase pitch as you increase the loudness.

CHILDREN CAN HELP TOO

Children can also play an important role in helping to check the hearing of brothers, sisters, and other children in the community.

▶ How to check babies 4 months and older

- Make a rattle from a can or gourd with small stones inside. A child can creep up quietly behind the baby. Make sure the baby does not see you first. Shake the rattle behind her head, first on one side and then the other. See if she is surprised.

- Call the baby's name from different places in the room. See if she responds in any way.

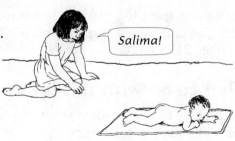

Salima!

▶ *Ways to check young children's hearing*
Game: What's that animal?

Make one child the speaker and have him stand 4 meters (12 feet) from a line of younger children. Behind each young child stands an older child with a pencil and paper.

speaker

cat

First, the speaker uses a very loud voice to say the name of a common animal.

The young children whisper the name they heard to their older partners. The older children write that down on a piece of paper.

Then the speaker names other animals, each one more quietly, until he is whispering. The older children write down every name that the young children tell them.

After the speaker has named about 10 animals, and the younger children's words have been written down, compare the lists. Any child who has not heard as many words as the others, or has not heard them correctly, may have a hearing problem.

Tests that can be done at a health center

A clinic or health center may also be able to test your child's hearing. This kind of testing can be useful if you think your child has difficulty hearing but you cannot tell what kinds of sounds he can hear, if any.

Unfortunately, a clinic that can test hearing may be very far away or be very expensive. But professional testing will be necessary if your child is going to use a hearing aid.

If you have already checked your child's hearing yourself in a familiar place, he may feel less afraid when he is tested by a strange person in a strange place. He may be more cooperative and he may understand more about what he is supposed to do.

Information from the hearing test is used to set a hearing aid to match the child's hearing. For more information about hearing aids see pages 217 to 224.

What to do with this information

If your child can hear some sounds, you can help her learn to use her hearing better. See the next chapter on developing listening skills. After working on your child's listening skills for about 6 months, check her hearing again to see if you get the same results.

Chapter 6

Listening skills

With help, children who cannot hear well can learn to listen more carefully to the sounds they are able to hear. Understanding more about sounds will help them learn more about their world and will help them use their hearing better, protect themselves, be safer, and become more able to take care of their own needs.

Some children can hear a little when people speak to them. Many children who cannot hear well may be able to hear loud noises, even if they cannot hear softer ones. Or they may hear a low-pitch sound like thunder, even if they cannot hear a high-pitch sound like a whistle. But because the sounds do not make sense to them, they do not pay attention to them.

If children practice listening, it will help them develop and use whatever hearing they may have.

To use his hearing better, a child must:

- notice sounds or voices.

- figure out the direction the sound or voice comes from.

- recognize what the sound is.

- tell the difference between sounds.

Manuel, listen to the chickens!

This chapter has activities that will encourage a child to look, to listen, and to feel the vibrations of sound. The activities will help children who cannot hear well learn more about sounds. The activities will also help you find out whether a child has some hearing, and what kind of sounds and words the child can hear. This information will help you know if it would be better for your child to learn a spoken language or a sign language.

As you do the activities in this chapter, look for signs that show the child is listening to a sound. She might show she is listening by turning her head, changing the look on her face, moving her body, getting very still, blinking her eyes, or making a sound herself.

Praise her if she responds to sounds and words. If she does not respond, repeat the sound if you can. Try moving the sound closer to her rather than making it louder. Be patient. It takes time for a child to develop listening skills.

As you practice listening, try to notice background noise. Even pleasant background sounds might keep a child from hearing your voice or picking out the one sound you want her to hear. If the child uses a hearing aid, remember that hearing aids make your voice louder but make other sounds louder too, including background noise.

Azlina heard some of her father's words. But because of the noise the other children are making, she is not sure exactly what he said.

Tips for parents

Try to become more aware yourself of the sounds around you. People who can hear often ignore sounds because they have become so familiar. They also know when to take more care, because they can recognize sounds that can mean danger.

Listening skills are important for all children who cannot hear well. Children will be safer if they learn to use whatever hearing they have.

Try to adapt the activities in this chapter so that your child is working with sounds she can hear. For example, if you know she can hear low-pitch sounds but not high ones, use sounds with low pitches when doing the activities. (See Chapter 5 for ways to learn what sounds your child can hear.) If you are not sure what sounds your child can hear, try different sounds.

ACTIVITIES

▶ *Ways to help your child notice sounds*

- When you hear a sound nearby, show your child that something is happening. Encourage her to look toward the sound.

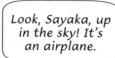

Look, Sayaka, up in the sky! It's an airplane.

- Let your child play with toys that make noise. From time to time, call her attention to the sound. If the toys do not make a lot of noise, tie something that makes noise, like a bell, onto the toy.

That's a loud noise, Radha!

- Find sounds you can start and stop. Let your child know that something is about to happen and then make the sound. Repeat the sound several times. Try pointing to your ear when a sound is made. This will help your child know when a sound is made.

- Make up games in which your child needs to listen to sounds in order to play.

While they hear the drum, the children dance.

When the music stops, everyone falls down.

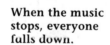

Some adults are not used to playing and may feel uncomfortable joining in activities with children. But music can help your child learn to use her hearing, and is a good way to involve other adults and children. Think of the songs you sang as a child, or learn songs that other children know. Choose songs that are happy, that have a nice rhythm, and that everybody can sing together. Adults and children can all be included. Make singing an everyday family activity.

► *Ways to help your child notice people's voices*

- Talk to your child as you hold her close. When she is touching your chest, neck, or cheek she will feel some vibration from the sound of your voice.

> You're getting to be such a big girl, Efra.

> Rub-a-dub-dub.

- As you do things with your child, make up sounds that go along with the activities.

- Say her name often.

> Juana! Come to me, Juana.

- When your child knows her name, use her name in songs and stories you make up. This will help catch her interest.

> Once there was a little girl named Seema...

- Talk with your child as often as you can. Use your voice in different ways. Try stretching words, and add high and low pitches. Use words that have opposite meanings.

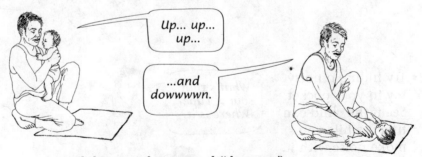

> Up... up... up...

> ...and dowwwwn.

A word that stretches a sound ('dowwwn') in contrast with an opposite short word ('up') gives sound clues that help young children understand.

▶ *How to learn the direction a sound comes from*

Children first learn to locate sounds that happen near their ears. Then they learn to look for the source of sounds that are above or below their ears. Then they look for the source of sounds that are farther and farther away. Finally, children learn to look for the source of sound that is behind them.

- If your child is interested in a noisy toy that you are sure she can hear, try moving it out of sight. Then make the noise again above her ears and see if she will turn her head to search for it. When she has learned to do this, make noise below the level of her ears. Finally, make a noise behind her.

Try to be patient, because it can take several months for a child to turn toward sounds. When she responds some of the time (even if not all the time), you can move on to the next step.

- Change the expression on your face, or call attention to the sound with a gesture — like pointing to your ear and then to what is making the sound.

- Try hiding a noisy toy in your pocket. See if the child can find it while you make noise with it.

What's that sound, Lupe? Where is it?

▶ *Ways to help your child recognize what a sound is*

- Notice common sounds that she hears and help her name them.

- When your child shows interest in a sound, explain what it is.

- Take your child to different places and when you hear sounds show her what is making them.

- Show her how to make different sounds herself.

▶ Ways to help your child notice when 2 sounds are different

- Find 2 things that make different sounds. Remember, they must have a pitch and loudness your child can hear. Put them in front of your child. Show her the noise each thing makes. Then ask her to close her eyes while you make a noise with one of the things. When she opens her eyes, ask her to show you which thing she thinks made the noise.

- Together, make up movements for 2 or 3 similar sounds. Then ask your child to make the movement whenever you make the sound. Here is an example with speech sounds:

Pa..pa..pa..pa.

La..la..la..la.

- Have your child guess who in the family is speaking by the sound of their voice. This will also help her learn to tell whether a man or woman is talking.

Who's talking now, Nami?

Is my child learning to listen?

You will need to do all these activities many times, over and over. After about 6 months, check your child's hearing again (see Chapter 5). You may find your child can hear more sounds than before. This does not mean her hearing has changed. It simply means she has learned to use her hearing better. Praise your child when she notices sounds and words.

As you practice together, try to build on what she has learned by using all the sounds she can hear. As a child learns more words and understands them better, she will be able to express herself better and be able to communicate more.

Chapter 7
Choosing and learning a language

When a child is comfortable using the basic communication skills described in Chapter 4, she is ready to learn a language. A child who is deaf or cannot hear well can first learn a sign language (see Chapter 8) or a spoken language (see Chapter 9). Whichever language a child learns, it must meet her needs.

The language she learns first will depend on many things such as how much she can hear, which language she prefers, her natural abilities and the resources available in her community. It can also depend on how her parents react to her deafness. Knowing deaf people in the community may help parents be able to accept their child's deafness and also find ways to help her learn a language.

In places where there are few resources for deaf children, parents might feel that they have no choice about which kind of language their child can learn. But if you put your child's needs and abilities first, you will make the best decisions you can.

It is not always easy to know
what is best for a child...
but you must try.

Learning language early is important

The best years for learning language are from birth to age 7. Usually a child learns most language between 2 and 4 years old. If a child does not learn language by the time he is about 7 or 8 years old, it will be more difficult for the child to learn it later. If a deaf child does not learn a spoken or a signed language, it will also be difficult for him to fully develop thinking skills. That is why learning language is so important.

How children learn language

Languages use symbols such as sounds, writing, or signs that allow people to communicate with each other. Reading, writing, speaking, and signing are all ways of using language.

The first step a child takes to learn language will be to learn the names for people and the words for things he sees every day — words like 'mama', 'cat', or 'baby'. But often, the first words he will say are to make something happen — words like 'milk', 'no', or 'up'.

Kofi, up.

A child learns that words have power to make things happen. It is very rewarding for a child to communicate and get what he wants.

Up, up, up, Adom!

Children first learn single words. Then they learn the rules for using words together. As they use language with other people, over time they learn the rules of language.

Children learn language by listening and seeing the language around them and practicing what they hear and see. Children develop their mental abilities when they learn more words and use them according to the language's rules. They make mistakes, and then begin to communicate successfully.

Grandma go-ed to the market?

Yes, Grandma went to the market.

Children learn language by practicing it with others.

LANGUAGE AND THINKING DEVELOP TOGETHER

Language allows us to communicate with others. It also allows us to communicate with ourselves. The language a child learns when he is young gives him the tools to develop his thinking — the language he uses to talk to himself. So even how we think depends on how much language we know and can use.

Daniel is deaf. He can communicate a little through gestures, expressions on his face, and through signs his family made up.

This is what Daniel can tell his mother about his day:

Fishing bad... little fish.

But if Daniel and his family shared a language, they could communicate much more. And Daniel's ability to think and plan would be stronger.

Today I went fishing, but I only caught little ones, about this long. I had to throw them back. Maybe tomorrow I will go fishing near the bridge.

The more children are able to learn a language — whether they speak or sign — the more they can understand their world, express themselves, think, hope, plan, and communicate with the people around them.

Children develop their thinking when:

- they see or hear people using words or signs to exchange information.

- they use language to describe what they see, hear, and touch.

- they use language to express what they experience.

- they use language to make connections between things.

The work will go quickly if we do it together.

Mayra develops her thinking skills by hearing people use language to express thoughts and ideas.

We got milk from that cow today!

Children develop thinking skills step-by-step

Please give me the big ball.

small ball, big ball

A young child first learns simple thinking skills by playing. For example, she learns the words 'small' and 'big'. Then she uses those words to understand that there is a 'small' ball, and a 'big' ball.

Then, when a child understands how to compare 'small' and 'big', she can begin to think about other things that are small or big. She learns the idea of 'size'.

The bigger shirt must be Papa's.

BASIC THINKING SKILLS AND LANGUAGE

As they learn language, children organize their thoughts and make connections between different ideas:

• how an object, person, or event causes something else to happen.

If I find wood for the fire, then Mama can cook dinner.

• how to solve problems.

I can reach the ball if I use a stick.

• how to order things one after the another.

First I add the egg. Then I mix in flour to make the dough sticky.

• how to count.

Papa is working tonight, so we need only 4 plates.

• how to identify categories of objects — to learn that one word can mean different things, and several words can mean the same thing.

This is a pineapple, that is a mango. Both are kinds of fruit.

• how to describe what a person is feeling and why she is feeling that way.

Mama is worried because Magda is so sick.

It is important that learning language becomes a part of the life of a child who is deaf or cannot hear well. Parents, community workers, and teachers must encourage children to learn and to use a language to express themselves, to communicate with others, and to develop their mental abilities.

Sign language and spoken language

The 2 kinds of language a child who is deaf or cannot hear well can learn are:

- **sign language,** when she uses her hands to communicate with the signs used by the deaf community in the region or country where she lives.

- **spoken language,** when she uses her voice and lip reading to communicate in the spoken language in that region or country.

Some children who can hear a little will be able to speak and read lips. Other children communicate best by making signs with their hands. You may want to begin with one language and teach your child other ways to communicate as he gets older.

For example:

Many people start with gestures and signs with a young child, especially if they are not sure if the child can hear speech sounds. Then, as the child gets older and understands some signs, they may try teaching her to read lips and to talk.

It's time to sleep.

Other people start with speaking and lip reading if they know their child can hear some sounds, or if he became deaf after he learned to talk. When a child is not learning a spoken language after a period of time, it may mean that a sign language is better suited for this child.

Vaw.

Ball! That's right!

The language your child uses may depend on:

- how much or how little he can hear.
- which language he prefers.
- how you react to his deafness.
- when he began to have difficulty hearing.
- the resources available in your family or community.

Using sign language

Sign language is used by deaf people throughout a community. It is a language that uses hand shapes, body movements, gestures, and expressions on the face to communicate experiences, thoughts, needs, and feelings. A sign language includes common gestures as well as thousands of signs that deaf people have developed over time.

> I want to be a teacher like you when I grow up!

> You would make a great teacher, Teresa.

Sign languages are real languages which have an organized grammar and structure just like spoken languages do. People use them to ask complicated questions, describe things around them, and discuss relationships, ideas, and beliefs. People use sign language to discuss how things affect each other, or refer to the past or the future. People who use a complete sign language can communicate everything that a hearing person can communicate using spoken words.

One way a sign language may be different from the local spoken language is that the order of signs in a sentence is often different from the order of spoken words.

For example, the question "What is your name?" would look like this in American Sign Language:

your

name

what?

Deaf people in nearly all countries, all over the world, have created their own complete sign languages. Like spoken languages, complete sign languages differ from region to region and country to country.

Here, for example, are the signs for 'mother' in 3 different countries:

Australia

Spain

Thailand

Even though they are different, each sign language is a full and natural way for deaf people to communicate.

BENEFITS OF USING SIGN LANGUAGE

- Young children learn sign language very easily when they are exposed to it. With practice, older children and teenagers are able to learn and use sign language without too much trouble.

- A child who uses sign language can communicate with anyone who knows the same sign language — just as fully as a hearing child who uses a spoken language. He will get to know other people who are deaf, and learn that deaf people are an important part of the community.

- It may be easier for a child who knows sign language to learn to read and write the language of her community. The more language a person has, the easier it is to learn another language.

- Unlike spoken languages, different sign languages are more easily understood by people around the world. It is easier for a signing child from China to communicate with a signing child from Nicaragua than it is for hearing people from those countries to communicate.

DIFFICULTIES WITH USING SIGN LANGUAGE

- A child who uses sign language cannot communicate with people who do not know sign language. To be able to communicate with your child, family members, friends, and others in the community must also learn sign language.

- While children learn to sign easily, adults have to study a lot to learn a complete sign language.

- If a family lives in a community where there are no people who use sign language, it may be very difficult to find a sign language teacher, or other people to use a sign language with.

Using spoken language

People who can hear communicate by talking, and hearing others talk, in their local language. It is natural for families to want their deaf child to understand their words and to talk to them using a spoken (oral) language.

To learn a spoken language, a child who cannot hear well will need to:

- listen with his remaining hearing so that he can learn to understand spoken words. It may be helpful for him to use a hearing aid.

- watch a person's lips when she is talking and guess the words she is saying (lip-reading).

- practice speaking words so that others will understand him better.

Remember, if you use spoken language with your child, you and your family will have to talk to your child as much as you can.

Boon.

Yes, Raimon, a spoon.

Be patient. Your child will learn language much more slowly than children who can hear well. You will need to make your child use words even when it is easier to do things for him or give him things without waiting for him to ask you.

Your child will speak differently. Most deaf children talk differently than a child who can hear. It is natural to feel embarrassed at first by the way your child speaks. Once you get used to it, you can explain this to other people.

This child is wearing hearing aids in a body harness.

Different communities have different ideas about how deaf children should learn to communicate. A pre-school in southern India tries to teach young children who cannot hear well to speak, read, write, and listen.

They try to prepare deaf children to attend regular schools at the age of 5. Because the school wants children not to be ashamed of being deaf, they insist that children wear body-harness hearing aids (see page 219). Besides making sounds louder, this sort of hearing aid helps everyone see and accept that these children are different.

BENEFITS OF USING SPOKEN LANGUAGE

- A child who communicates like other people in the community will have many more people who understand him.

- A child who uses a spoken language will be more ready for a school if that school does not use sign language.

- A child using spoken language may find it easier to read, because the language he speaks and the written language are similar.

I am glad Haipeng is going to a nursery school where he can talk with other children who cannot hear well.

Yes, and I hope it will prepare him to attend the regular school later. I want him to study so he can get a good job when he grows up!

DIFFICULTIES WITH USING SPOKEN LANGUAGE

- Spoken communication usually works well only for a child who has some hearing (enough to hear the differences between many words) or for a child who became deaf after he had learned to speak.

- A child may find it difficult to read lips, because many sounds look the same on the lips or cannot be seen on the lips. For example, the words 'baby', 'maybe', and 'pay me' all look the same. You can see this yourself in a mirror.

The words 'baby', 'maybe', and 'pay me' all look the same on the lips.

- A child who has difficulty hearing speech sounds will find it very difficult to speak clearly, because he cannot hear himself talk. His speech may not be understood by anyone but his family.

- Young children may not sit still for long lessons to teach language.

- Because so much effort goes into learning to talk and learning to understand what other people are saying, a child may miss learning more about the world.

Things to think about

Because each family — and each child — has different needs and abilities, there is no single method that is always right for everyone. The important thing is to work well with the resources you have. The next few pages give some information and ask some questions that can help you get the best results with your child.

SIGN LANGUAGE

may succeed if:

- your family is able and willing to learn and use sign language.

- there are people or books that can teach sign language to your child and your family.

- there is a deaf school in your area that teaches sign language to students.

is **more likely** to succeed if:

- your family is patient and everyone works hard to learn and use sign language.

- there are people who can teach a complete local sign language to your child and your family.

SPOKEN LANGUAGE

may succeed if:

- your child can hear some speech sounds (see Chapter 4, 'Finding out what your child can hear').

- your child learned to speak and understand words before he lost his hearing.

- your child finds it easy to read lips (some children are better at it than others).

is **more likely** to succeed if:

- your child has a hearing aid that he uses almost all the time.

- your child gets professional help at a clinic or pre-school program for deaf children.

How many people will your child be able to communicate with?

It is important for children who cannot hear well to communicate with many other people. A child who uses home signs can communicate with only the people in his home. A child who uses a more complete sign or spoken language will be able to communicate with more people. A child who can also read and write the local spoken language will be able to communicate with many more people.

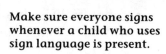

Whether you use a spoken or sign language, it is very important that the whole family use it together. This way your child can communicate with everyone in the family. He will also feel included in the

Make sure everyone signs whenever a child who uses sign language is present.

family and can learn about the world from their conversations.

People without hearing problems can learn sign language if they want to. The story on page 150 tells how people in a town in Brazil learned to communicate with deaf children.

What if your child's first language is not your language?

Using the same language helps communication. But often the sign language used by deaf children to develop their minds and learn about the world is not the language used by their families. Many parents and deaf children who use different languages find it difficult to communicate with each other. They may not feel close to each other and become frustrated because it is so hard to understand each other. Deaf children may feel left out in the family home.

Sign language may be best for the child but less convenient for the family. Or it may draw attention to a child who communicates in a different way. But with the support of their communities, parents of deaf children can help their children learn the language that is right for them.

I feel so happy now that I can use sign language with Amadou.

And we can help his cousins learn to sign, too.

When did your child begin to have difficulty hearing?

If your child became deaf after he learned to speak, he may still be able to read people's lips and improve his speech. He can continue to develop his language even after he loses his hearing. But if your child is born completely deaf or cannot hear speech sounds, it will be very difficult or impossible for him to learn to read lips or to speak.

Children who learned to talk before they lost their hearing can speak better than children who were born deaf.

This boy lost some hearing at age 3. He can hear some speech sounds. He may learn to speak and read lips.

This girl became deaf when she was 6. She can speak and read lips.

These children were born deaf. They cannot speak or read lips.

How much can your child hear?

The more speech sounds (talking) a child can hear, the more he can use his hearing to understand words or parts of words, to read lips, and perhaps to learn to speak. Children who cannot hear speech sounds will have difficulty learning these skills or may never learn them.

This child can hear speech sounds. She might learn to read lips and to speak.

This child cannot hear any sounds at all. It will be very difficult or impossible for her to read lips or to speak.

What's that, Safiya?

What do you have, Abena?

Will your child use a hearing aid?

A hearing aid may help your child understand words. But hearing aids do not help all children. Sometimes health professionals may suggest that your child use a hearing aid. Try to get opinions from other parents with children who wear hearing aids, and remember

that each child's hearing is different. If you think you want to buy hearing aids for your child, read pages 217 to 224 to help you decide.

The people who sell hearing aids may give you some information about them. But they are not always the best people to ask for advice. They may be more interested in selling their products than about finding out what is right for your child. Sometimes the clinic or the hearing aid store may allow the child to use the hearing aid for a few days or weeks before deciding to buy it.

This is the best brand of hearing aid. Of course it will help your child.

A hearing aid may help your child. But it may not. Do not let anyone pressure you into buying something or make you feel guilty if you do not.

How will I know if my child is learning?

It will take time to know if a child is learning a language. After you have worked with a language for several months or more, evaluate how your child is doing. Ask yourself these questions:

• Does my child understand more than she did before?

• Is my child using speech or sign more often than before?

• Does she seem interested in learning to communicate? Or is she getting more and more frustrated?

• Does my child have any behavior problems that may be caused by frustration with not knowing a language, or with not knowing it enough to understand and express herself?

• Do I enjoy communicating with my child, or is it always a frustrating experience?

• Can we communicate easily enough so that I am able to talk with my child about what is happening?

• Does my child communicate well with other people?

• Can my child understand the information that her brothers and sisters understand?

Parents are often told they must choose one language to communicate with their child and keep using it, no matter how much or how little their child is learning. Sometimes health workers encourage this, because they think one method is right and the others are wrong. But no method is perfect.

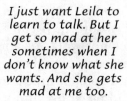

I just want Leila to learn to talk. But I get so mad at her sometimes when I don't know what she wants. And she gets mad at me too.

Let's not get discouraged. We can work together to find some new ways to help her.

If your child is not learning and is getting very frustrated, then try another approach. Each family must make their own decision based on their child's hearing and their situation.

Who knows what is best for your child?

Many people have strong opinions about what language to use with deaf children. In many countries, using spoken language (oral communication) with deaf children has been the rule for many years. Sometimes, medical and education professionals tell you that **all** deaf children can learn to speak. This is not true, even though they may introduce you to a child who is deaf and who speaks perfectly.

All children can learn to talk if you spend enough time practicing with them.

Sometimes professionals tell you what they themselves were taught many years ago. They may tell you that you must use spoken language with your child or you are not being responsible. This is not true. You know your child and family situation better than they do.

But I already spend all the time I can with Marta — and she still does not respond when I speak to her. And my other children and my sick mother need me too.

Maybe sign language would work better...

Use the language that works for your child

Your child needs to express himself and understand others. A child needs to know more than to say 'mama' or 'papa'. He needs to develop the ability to listen, to understand what is said, and to respond and communicate with others as easily and as fully as possible.

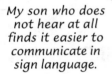

My grandson uses over 500 words now!

Parents and caregivers can help a child learn language in a way that makes it possible for him to absorb it. If you find that sign language does not work for your child, think about helping him learn a spoken language. Or if he does not seem to understand spoken language, try to help him learn sign language. Once children know and use one language well, it will be easier for them to learn another language.

Talking to parents whose children have learned a language — a sign language or a spoken language, or both — will help other parents who are trying to teach their children a language.

My son who does not hear at all finds it easier to communicate in sign language.

*But some deaf children **can** learn to understand words and talk. My child did.*

Even if they cannot hear words, deaf children can still learn to use written language. A child who is deaf learns how words look, rather than how they might sound. They see the relationships between symbols. (This is also how the written Chinese language works.) Deaf children who learn to use a language early — a spoken or a signed language — can learn to read and write well. It will help if they also meet deaf adults who can read.

Sometimes deaf people do not learn to communicate when they are children. Although it is much better for young children to learn communication, older children and even adults can learn to communicate. Chapters 8 and 9 describe methods you can use to teach a language to children who are deaf or cannot hear well.

- To help a child learn a sign language, see Chapter 8.

- To help a child learn a spoken language, see Chapter 9.

Resources that can help

How children who are deaf or cannot hear well learn a language will depend on the child, the resources available, the families and caregivers, and their communities. But it will be easier for parents and caregivers to help children learn a language if they get support from each other, from community organizations, from schools for the deaf, or from other organizations.

Resources in the community can include:

- a deaf community in your area, deaf clubs, or someone who can teach your child and your family sign language.
- community-based rehabilitation programs, parents' groups, and other community-based groups.
- teachers in local schools, older deaf children, or others who are willing to try to teach your deaf child.
- a school in your community that can teach deaf children.
- books and videos about issues and themes of importance to deaf people, experience of life as a deaf person, and stories about successful deaf people.

Learning to sign will also help your child get to know other people who are deaf. She will learn that deaf people are an important part of the community.

If there are deaf adults in your community, ask them to spend time with your family and to teach you all to sign.

Mama, now you can sign just like me and Alfredo!

My name is Esme.

Good! Now both of you repeat after me...

If there are no deaf people in your area, try to contact your country's Association of the Deaf, or a school for deaf children. Try to get books to help you learn to sign. If this is not possible, continue to use local signs and gestures, and create more signs of your own.

The important thing is that you communicate as much as possible with your child. Most of all, children need people to love them, encourage them, and give them direction. This will help language become a part of children's lives.

Your child should know that your love and approval do not depend on his ability to speak or sign.

Chapter 8
Learning to use
a sign language

It is easy for a young child to learn a complete sign language. A child will first begin to understand the signs that others use, especially for people and things that she sees every day. After she begins to use signs that are important to her, she will learn and use many others.

Each sign will help your child learn more about the world around her. As her language skills develop, she will begin to put signs together. After a while she will be able to sign in full sentences. This will also help her develop her mind. If you and your child enjoy learning sign language together, you will get better results.

Drink?

The best way for you and your family to learn the sign language used in your area is to have a deaf person who uses it teach you. See Chapter 3 for guidelines on how to teach your child language. See pages 103 and 150 for more information on how deaf adults can help the community learn sign language.

If there is no one who can teach sign language, there may be a book to learn some signs to use with your child. But learning sign language from a book is harder and less effective than learning from a person.

In this chapter, we show people using signs, and we also show how signs can be put together to make **sign sentences**, like this:

One picture by itself does not show all of the signs in a sentence.

Say hello to Papa.

hello

Papa

We sometimes show the signs that make up a sentence in boxes that you read from top to bottom.

▶ How to help your child understand new signs

A child first learns the signs for things and people that are important
to her. So notice who or what your child is interested in. To help a
child learn her first signs:

1. It helps to make the sign near the object
   or point to the person, so your child
   connects the
   two. Show by
   the look on
   your face that
   something important
   is happening.

*Say hello
to Papa.*

hello

Papa

2. Sign the name of the object or person
   and use it several times. **Be sure
   your child can see your hands and
   face when you sign with her.**

*Hello,
Papa.*

*Hello,
Norma!*

3. Watch for your child's response.
   Does she respond in any way
   that shows she understood? If so,
   praise her. If she does not
   respond, repeat the sign a few
   more times.

4. Use these signs as much
   as you can throughout
   the day. Encourage the
   whole family to use
   them, too.

   Try to be patient. It may
   take your child some
   time to learn her first
   signs.

Papa.

*This is Papa's
chair. For Papa.*

Help your child learn different kinds of signs

In addition to learning the names of objects and people, your child needs to learn many different kinds of signs. This will help her learn more about the world around her. it will also prepare her to be able to think and sign in sentences later on.

You can use the same steps as on the previous page to teach your child '**action** signs', '**feeling** signs', and '**describing** signs'.

- **action** signs

Signs for 'eat', 'sleep', and 'drink' are often the first action signs a child learns.

Eat your soup, Thuy.

eat

soup

- **feeling** signs

Signs for 'happy', 'sad', and 'angry' are often the first feeling signs a child learns.

*You look **sad**, Ramona.*

- **describing** signs

Signs for 'wet', 'dry', 'hot', or 'cold' are often the first describing signs a child learns.

Hot?

*Stay back, Seema. The pan is **hot**.*

pan

hot

Another kind of sign that is important to know is:

- **name** signs (the name given to each person)

You can make up name signs for each member of the family. A sign will be easier to remember if it looks like the person in some way. This brother and sister made up signs for each other based on how they look:

Learning to sign

When your child sees people around her using sign language to communicate she will begin to use signs herself. Remember that some signs are easier to use than others.

When a child learns to sign, she first learns where to put her hands. Then she learns to move her hands in the right way and, finally, to shape her hand and fingers correctly.

This shape is easier. This shape is more difficult.

Your child is not going to make every sign exactly right. At first, you may not even be able to understand the sign. But praise her for trying, and do not be too anxious about her signing clearly.

▶ *Ways to encourage your child to begin using signs*

1. Watch for the messages she is already sending through gestures, sounds, and expressions on the face.

2. Give her the sign for the message she is sending.

Drink.

3. Emphasize the sign, and repeat it several times. Encourage her to imitate you.

   If she tries to imitate you, praise her. If she does not make the sign in the right way, do not correct her. Instead, simply repeat the correct sign.

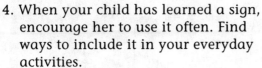

Drink?

That's right, Fatima, drink!

4. When your child has learned a sign, encourage her to use it often. Find ways to include it in your everyday activities.

Dolly drinks!

Ask questions that can be
answered with a single sign.

Do you want
your doll or
blanket?

want

doll

blanket

Doll.

If your child answers, praise her. If
your child does not answer:

• she may not understand the sign.

• she may not understand the idea
of a question — that it needs an
answer.

One way to teach your child about questions is to answer them for
her at first. After a while she will get the idea.

How many squash
do we need?

Squash?

We need
2 squash.

► How to encourage your child to communicate simple needs

When your child wants something, she is more eager to learn a sign that will help her get what she wants. Here are some ideas for encouraging your child to use sign language to communicate simple needs:

What do you want, Rani? Tell me in sign language.

- Whenever your child seems to want something, encourage her to sign for what she wants.

- Create situations that need your child to ask for something.

Play more?

Oscar's father stopped their game until Oscar asked him to continue.

When your child uses a gesture that can mean different things, act confused. Encourage her to send a more specific message by giving you the sign.

Do you want your cup or ball?

Can you sign 'cup'?

Cup.

▶ *How to help your child make and follow simple requests*

As your child learns to recognize the names of objects, people, and activities, she can begin to understand simple requests you make. Begin with short requests. Emphasize the signs she already knows and use gestures to make the message more clear. Be sure to give your child enough time to respond and repeat the request if necessary.

At first, make requests about objects or people she can see around her.

Ai, bring me your shirt.

bring

your

shirt

Then make requests about objects or people she cannot see, using signs you have taught her.

Ai, bring me some water, please.

Your child will soon learn to make requests herself. Everyone should encourage her when she tries to make requests.

Play?

Yes, come play with us, Jama.

▶ Ways to encourage your child to learn more signs

The best way to help your child learn more signs is to communicate with her as much as you can — and to encourage her to send messages back to you. Here are a few ideas for communicating throughout the day.

- Everyday activities are a good time to learn new signs. This gives a child a chance to use the same signs over and over.

  Always make sure your child is looking at you when you sign with her.

What goes on next, Mei Mei? Your pants?

Pants.

your

pants

- Make a mistake to encourage your child to correct you. Here, this child's mother called her by her brother's name.

Who's this for? Is it for Raj?

No! Neela!

Try making up games that include some new signs. For example, these children are playing a game to find hidden objects they can name by sign. At the same time they are learning some new signs.

See if you can find the cup, bottle, spoon, and can.

Understanding groups of signs

After using single signs, a child begins to put signs together to express complete thoughts. By learning to combine signs to express complete thoughts, a child is on the way to using a full language.

Putting groups of signs together is a big step for a child. It allows him to communicate more about the objects and people around him than just their names. At first he puts 2 signs together. Then he begins to use 3 signs — and, finally, longer groups of signs. He must first understand how other people do this before he can do it himself.

▶ *How to help your child understand groups of signs*

1. When your child names an object or person, expand on what he says.

Tree.

Stress the group of signs you want your child to learn and repeat it several times.

This is a **big tree**.
It is a very **big tree**!

2. Watch for your child's response. Does he respond in any way that shows he understood? If so, praise him. If he does not respond, repeat the sign several times.

That's right, a **big tree**.

3. Use these signs as much as you can throughout the day. Encourage the whole family to use them too.

Remember the **big tree**, Manop? Tell Mama about the **big tree**.

remember

big

tree

In this example, the parents put together the name of an object ('tree') with a word that describes it ('big').

Knowing words and using a language helps a child develop his mind. When he knows words like 'big' and 'small', he can use those words to think and to express difficult ideas — like comparing one thing to another. See Chapter 7 for information about how language helps a child's mind to develop.

To teach your child other groups of signs, try putting the name of an object or person together with:

- a word or sign that shows what a person or thing does.

*Look how you made Auntie Vijaya **laugh**.*

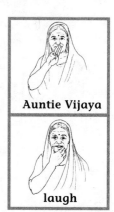

Auntie Vijaya

laugh

- a word or sign that shows where an object or person is.

*Now you can stay warm **under** the blanket, Adwin.*

- a word or sign that shows wanting more, or for something to happen again.

*Do you want **more** rice?*

want

more

- a word or sign that shows not wanting something, that something is all gone, or that something cannot be done.

*No, Salim, the sweets are **all gone**.*

Using groups of signs

You have been using groups of signs to communicate with your child. For a child to begin using groups of signs by himself, he needs to know several signs so he can put them together in different ways.

▶ *Ways to encourage your child to put signs together*

When your child signs a single sign, encourage him to expand on what he says. You could:

- expand on the sign yourself and encourage him to copy you.

Can you sign 'big tree'?

Big tree!

- ask a question and encourage her to answer.

That is a pretty necklace, Maryam! Who gave it to you?

- ask your child about what he is doing.

What are you making, Minh?

House.

What are you making it with?

Sticks and leaves.

making

what

Here are some more ways to encourage your child to use groups of signs:

- Ask your child to deliver a simple message.

Tell Papa, 'come eat'.

- Try telling stories together. When your child has seen you tell a story many times, he may be able to sign part of it himself.

Three goats were walking down the road... Who did the goats meet?

Brother fox.

- Encourage your child to take on different roles.

Now you be Mama for a while.

What does Mama do?

Mama cooks.

▶ Use questions to encourage your child to think

Asking questions is a good way to keep communication going. Questions also encourage your child to think.

- Give your child tasks that ask her to think in new ways. Then encourage her to communicate about what she is doing.

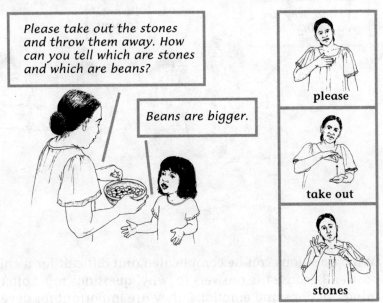

Please take out the stones and throw them away. How can you tell which are stones and which are beans?

Beans are bigger.

please

take out

stones

- When your child has a problem, ask her to tell you how to solve it.

The wagon is too heavy to pull. What should we do?

what

we

do?

- When you notice your child is expressing an emotion, ask her to explain how she feels.

If she has trouble answering you, first think about whether she knows the signs she needs to answer the question. If she does not, help her learn these signs.

> Li Ming, why are you crying?

> I want to play.

'Why' questions can be complicated and difficult for a child to answer. Because the answers to 'why' questions must often include things, actions and emotions, they are important for developing children's thinking skills. A child needs a lot of practice to answer these questions, so keep working on 'why' questions. If your child still has trouble answering the question, give her several choices.

> Li Ming, you look upset. Are you feeling sad? Or angry?

> Sad.

▶ How to help your child follow 2-step requests

When your child understands more signs, he can begin to follow more difficult requests. You can start by expanding the simple requests your child already understands, by turning them into requests with 2 steps.

First, make a request about something your child can see.

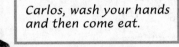

Carlos, wash your hands and then come eat.

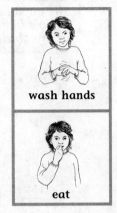

wash hands

eat

Then slowly make the requests more difficult.

Carlos, after you eat, please bring some firewood from outside.

▶ Help your child notice that how a sign is made is part of its meaning

A person adds meaning to her signs by making them larger or smaller, by making some signs slower or faster than others, and by changing the way her face looks.

Help your child pay attention to these different ways of signing so he will understand more of the message being sent.

If you want to say something is bad, you can make a sign like this:

bad

If you want to say it is very bad, you would make the same sign ('bad') larger and faster:

very bad

Telling stories is one of the most enjoyable ways to teach your child sign language. Try signing in different ways as you play different characters. Also try putting a lot of emotion (like joy or sadness) in your voice and on your face to show how the characters are feeling.

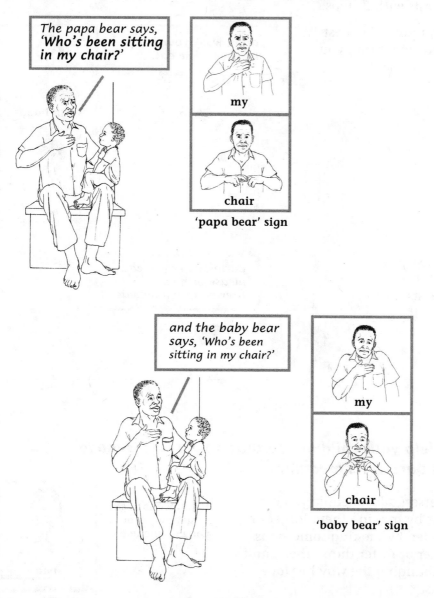

The papa bear says, 'Who's been sitting in my chair?'

my

chair

'papa bear' sign

and the baby bear says, 'Who's been sitting in my chair?'

my

chair

'baby bear' sign

Signing for different characters helps a child pay attention to the story. It also helps a child see the expression, the size, and the different ways signs are made.

Teaching sign language to parents of deaf children

People who use sign language as their first language can teach parents how to communicate with babies and children who are deaf.

Here is a story about a group of Indian mothers with deaf children, living in England, who learned British sign language from a deaf teacher. Before they learned sign language, the children and their parents had trouble communicating because it was so hard to understand each other. Learning sign language changed this.

Signing across language barriers

Lisa is a British woman who was born deaf. After she finished teacher training school, she got a job teaching deaf children. Part of her job was to help the mothers of the deaf children learn sign language. Among the groups that Lisa taught was a group of Indian women who did not speak English. At first, it was difficult for Lisa and the mothers to communicate with each other. Lisa used British sign language and another teacher translated for her into spoken English. Then another woman translated the spoken English into Punjabi, the language that all the mothers spoke.

I am so glad Ashis and I can share ideas with each other now...

The mothers' group first learned signs about the home. They also learned signs for what the children were studying in class. This helped parents understand and communicate with their child at home.

Later, a man joined Lisa's group of mothers learning to sign. He then taught fathers and older brothers in a group for men. In both groups, parents with older deaf children shared their experience with parents of very young deaf children. This let them use their new sign language skills to talk about things that were very important to them.

Watching Lisa work and teach, the parents saw that deaf children could be teachers, make a living, and be respected by other people. Many families in the community learned something about deaf people at the same time that they learned how to communicate with their deaf children.

TIPS FOR ADULTS LEARNING SIGN LANGUAGE

Sign language depends a lot on the way you express things through the whole body. The way you stand, and expressions on your face all communicate as much as your hands.

See how Nimi's expression changes as she asks the question, "What should we do?" in sign language.

| what | we | do |

Deaf people watch the face of the person they are communicating with — not only that person's hands — just as hearing people look at each other's faces as they listen.

- Act out what you want to say. Do not worry about making mistakes or looking foolish.

- Use anything and everything that helps to communicate: gestures, expressions on the face, body movements, pointing, signing, and finger spelling (spelling out words by using signs for each letter). Try communicating an idea or simple sentence with no formal signs at all. Just use gestures, facial expression, and pointing. Even when you do not know or forget a formal sign, you can still communicate with deaf people this way.

> *Minh and I sometimes make each other laugh trying to act out a sign we do not know. But the more we sign, the more we learn!*

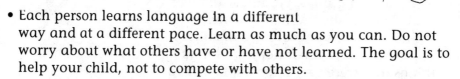

- Each person learns language in a different way and at a different pace. Learn as much as you can. Do not worry about what others have or have not learned. The goal is to help your child, not to compete with others.

- To really learn sign language, use it often with deaf people who sign.

Learning sign language will not be easy. But remember, it is important to your child to have a common language that all of you can share. Keep practicing sign language. If you do not use it, you lose it — just like any other language you learn.

Chapter 9
Learning to use a spoken language

Children who can hear the differences between many words or who became deaf after they learned to speak may be able to use a spoken language.

Most deaf children talk differently from children who can hear. People who do not know a particular deaf child well often have difficulty understanding her speech. If you use a spoken language with your child, she will need extra help as she learns to read lips and speak clearly. You will get better results if you and your child enjoy learning words and language together. Remember, everyone in the home will have to talk to your child as much as possible.

First, a child will begin to understand words that other people use. Then your child will begin to use words for people and things she sees every day that are important to her. Later she will learn many different kinds of words. This will help your child learn to speak in sentences. See Chapter 3 for guidelines on how to teach your child language.

▶ How to get your child's attention

Your child needs to see your lips move to be able to understand your words. Be sure she is looking at you when you talk to her.

If your child responds to her name, use it to get her attention. If she does not respond, try tapping the floor with your foot, so she feels the vibration.

► Ways to keep your child's interest

- Talk about things she knows and can see: her food, her clothing, her toys.

- Talk about things that interest her. If she likes trucks, talk about them. If she likes to play with dolls, talk about what she is doing.

- Talk often, not just at teaching times. Your child may not yet understand the words, but it will help her become more aware of language.

Face your child when you are talking, and be in good light so she can see your face.

- Try to reduce the noise around you. Remember to speak close to the child. If her hearing in one ear is better, remember to speak near that ear.

► How to help your child learn speech sounds

Simply speaking to a child who can hear is enough for him to be able to learn to speak. But to help a child who cannot hear well learn to speak, he needs to listen to and remember the distinct speech sounds that make up words. So in addition to talking naturally to your child, you should have your child listen to and use specific speech sounds.

Every language has sounds that are easier and harder for children to learn. Teach the simpler sounds first (like 'ma' before 'ra').

It's _cold_. C-c-c-_cold_. You need a _coat_.

Every 2 weeks, choose a different distinct speech sound and and use it as often as you can — in conversation, by itself, or as a game. Ask other people to use the same speech sound too.

Repeat the chosen sound as often as you can. Use the speech sound alone too, for example, by saying 'c-c-c cold'.

▶ *How to help your child learn his first words*

Your child will have to learn to watch your lips and listen very carefully. So it is best to teach only a few words at a time.

Watch your own lips in a mirror, or watch other people's lips when they talk, to see what kinds of sounds can be seen on your lips. Sometimes different sounds look the same on the lips. You will soon see how hard it can be to read lips.

The words 'baby', 'maybe', and 'pay me' all look the same on the lips.

To help a child learn a word:

1. Choose a few words that are easy to see on the lips. Some sounds are easier to see than others. Sounds like 'b' where the lips start to close and then open are the easiest to see.

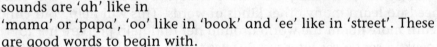

Let's play **ball**. Give me the **ball**.

2. Choose words that are easy to hear. Some sounds are louder than others. Some of the loudest sounds are 'ah' like in 'mama' or 'papa', 'oo' like in 'book' and 'ee' like in 'street'. These are good words to begin with.

3. It is easiest to hear a word if it is at the beginning or end of a sentence.

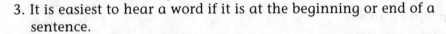

4. To teach words, you will have to use them hundreds of times. So choose words that can be used in conversation many times every day.

Now I'll roll the ball.

Ba.

5. Use the same words over and over in the same situations. Repeating them is necessary, and young children like it.

6. Speak clearly. Use careful, but not exaggerated, lip movements.

7. Make a short list of useful words you want your child to learn, and ask everyone in the family to use them often. Choose words that are easy to see on the lips.

Everybody should use the same word for anything that can have different names — like 'coat' or 'jacket'.

> Put on your coat.

> Put on your coat now.

When you are sure your child understands the words you have been using, teach more words that look and sound very different from the first few words. As you teach your child the new words, continue to practice the old words.

YOUR CHILD NEEDS TO KNOW DIFFERENT KINDS OF WORDS

In addition to learning the names of objects and people, your child needs to learn many other kinds of words. This will help your child learn more about the world around her and help prepare her to speak in sentences later on. Be sure to practice all of the following:

• **proper names**
(the name given
to each person)

> *Nisa* and *Moshe* are here. Let's say hello to them.

• **action** words

Rrrrr...

Yes, you can **ride** the scooter just like Papa!

• **describing** words

You were right. The baby was **hungry**. She cries when she is hungry.

• **feeling** words

You look **happy**! Are you happy to see your little brother?

Knowing '**name** words', '**action** words', '**describing** words', and '**feeling** words' helps a child to use those words to think about the world around her.

When children know the meanings of words, they can learn to compare, sort and order things, solve problems, and describe feelings. See Chapter 7 for more information on how children develop their language and thinking.

▶ How to encourage your child to begin using words

If your child has difficulty hearing speech sounds, he can learn to watch your lips to give him clues about how to say these words himself. It is important to remember, though, that many sounds look the same on the lips.

1. Encourage children to use words when playing. Sit in front of the child in good light and show him something that interests him, like a favorite toy. Encourage him to watch your lips move as you say the name of the toy. Repeat the same word several times.

2. Have the child try to copy you.

Be sure to speak clearly and in a natural way. This will help your child read the lips of other people saying the same thing.

3. Sit with the child in front of a mirror, so she can see both of your faces. Show her an object. Say the name of the object, and then have her copy you.

4. Repeat these steps with different words, especially ones that name things your child is interested in at the moment.

Your child is not going to say words exactly right. Remember, she cannot hear exactly how the words are supposed to sound. At first, you may not even be able to understand what word she is saying. But praise her for trying, and do not be too anxious about having your child say words clearly.

▶ *Encourage your child to communicate simple needs*

When your child wants something, she is more eager to learn a word that will help her get what she wants.

- Whenever your child seems to want something, encourage her to ask for what she wants using words.

▶ *How to encourage your child to answer simple questions*

Asking your child questions is a good way to encourage her to talk. Remember to use looks on the face (like raising your eyebrows and looking puzzled) and body movements (like tilting your head) to help your child know you are asking a question.

- To begin, try asking questions that require a 'yes' or 'no' answer. When your child shakes her head 'yes' or 'no', remind her to use the word that sends the same message.

- Ask questions that can be answered with a single word.

If your child answers, praise him. If your child does not answer:

- he may not understand the words you are using.

- he may not understand that a question needs an answer.

You can teach your child about questions by answering them for her at first. After a while she will get the idea.

- Create situations that need your child to ask for something. Here, Ana's sister gave her an empty bowl and waited for her to ask for beans.

▶ Help your child pay attention to how words are said

Whenever people speak, they tend to stress some words more than others (loudness), to speak some words more quickly than others (rhythm), and to change how high or deep their voices are (pitch). People also show what they are feeling by their tone of voice. These different ways of speaking all add meaning to the message being sent.

Listening to the tone in his mother's voice and her stress on the word 'no' helps Manuel know what she means.

▶ *How to help your child say things in different ways*

Just as your child learns to listen and watch for the different ways things are said, he needs to learn to speak in different ways.

- Play games that encourage your child to speak with feeling.

- Encourage your child to sing. This will help his voice go up and down, and help change the rhythm of his speech.

▶ How to help your child follow simple requests

As your child learns to recognize the names of objects, people, and
activities, he can begin to understand simple requests you make.
Begin with short requests. Emphasize the words he already knows,
and use gestures to make the message more clear. Be sure to give
your child enough time to respond. Repeat the request if necessary.

At first, make requests about
objects or people he can see
around him.

Then make requests about
objects or people he cannot see.

Chin, put your
shirt on.

Get your sandals,
Haseeb. You need
to wear sandals
when you go
outside.

▶ Ways to encourage your child to learn more words

The best way to help your child learn more words is to communicate
with her as much as you can — and to encourage her to speak to
you. Here are a few ideas for communicating often throughout the
day:

• Everyday activities are
a good time to learn
new words. This gives
a child a chance to
practice the same
words over and over.

Is that your
knee, Manu?
Your knee?

• Make a mistake to encourage her to correct you.

• Leave out a word in a song or nursery rhyme your child has heard often. Encourage him to say the missing word.

After using single words, a child begins to put words together to express complete thoughts. At first he puts 2 words together. Then he begins to use 3 words — and finally, bigger groups of words.

Putting groups of words together is a big step for a child. It allows him to say more about the objects and people around him. He must first learn to understand how other people do this before he begins to do it himself.

Understanding groups of words used by others

▶ How to help your child understand groups of words

1. When your child names an object or person, expand on what he says.

   Stress the group of words you want your child to learn and repeat the group several times.

2. Praise your child if he responds in any way that shows he understood. If he does not respond, repeat the words several times.

3. Use these words as much as you can throughout the day. Encourage the whole family to use them, too.

In this example, the parents put together the name of an object (eggs) with a word that describes it (chicken). Using a group of words in a full sentence can help focus a child's attention on the words.

To teach your child other groups of words, try putting the name of an object or person together with:

- a word that shows what a person or thing does.

- a word that shows who or what an object belongs to.

- a word that shows where an object or person is.

- a word that shows someone wants something to happen again.

- a word that shows something is over, or that something cannot be done.

*Fish **swim**.*

***Papa's** shirt.*

*Maria is **on** the swing.*

*Do you want **more** beans?*

*Rice is **finished**.*

▶ How to help your child follow 2-step requests

When your child understands more words, he can begin to follow more difficult requests. You can begin by expanding the simple requests your child already understands by turning them into requests that have 2 steps.

Pick the beans and put them in the basket.

Then slowly make the requests more difficult.

Chin, can you empty the basket and bring it back?

Learning to use groups of words

For a child to begin using groups of words by himself, he needs to know several words so he can put them together in different ways.

▶ Ways to encourage your child to put words together

When your child says a single word, encourage him to expand on what he says. You could:

- expand on the words yourself and encourage him to copy you.

- ask a question and encourage him to answer.

Push!

Say 'push more'.

Do you want to push high? Can you say 'push high'?

Here are some more ideas for encouraging your child to use groups of words:

- Ask your child about what she is doing.

- When your child has a problem, ask him to tell you how to solve it.

- Ask your child to deliver a simple message.

- Try telling stories together. When your child has heard and seen a story many times, she may be able to tell part of it herself.

• Encourage your child to act out different roles.

• Praise him when he puts words together. By using complete sentences, expand on what he says. Talk to him in complete sentences. But do not expect him to use complete sentences yet.

• Share the ideas or feelings you are thinking about as you play together.

Keep practicing the spoken language. Remember, it is important for your child to have a language that all of you can share.

Chapter 10

Social skills

When people get along well with others, it means they have good 'social skills'. People develop social skills as they relate to each other, learn about themselves, and consider other people's feelings.

Having good social skills is important for everyone. To be part of any group — whether a family, a group of friends, or even a class at school — it is necessary to have social skills.

Social skills are more than just good manners. Good social skills let people:

• give and receive attention, affection, or help.

• express their needs, feelings, and rights in an acceptable way.

• communicate effectively.

It is important for children who are deaf or cannot hear well to develop good social skills. Their ability to get along with other people will help them be less isolated.

Like hearing children, deaf children must develop social skills by watching and interacting with the people around them. This helps them learn to do things like treating older people with respect, asking permission to use things that belong to someone else, or waiting for their turn to participate in an activity.

Good social skills will help children make friends and relate to others in the community.

How children learn social skills

We are not born with social skills. We begin to learn them as babies, as soon as we become aware of other people. As children and adults, we continue to learn and use these skills throughout our lives.

At first these social skills are very simple. A baby learns to return his mother's smile or a child learns to take turns while playing a game. But as a child grows older, he needs more developed social skills to get along with other people.

2 years old

- asks others when she needs help
- plays alongside other children
- imitates caregiver

3 years old

- enjoys helping around the house
- likes to be praised for doing simple tasks
- is aware of other people's feelings

5 years old

- understands rules, and ideas like fairness and right and wrong
- expresses many feelings
- plays with other children

The 'right' behavior for your child depends on his age. If you expect more than your child can do, you and he will both be unhappy. But if you expect too little from your child, he will not learn new skills. For more information on when children learn new social skills, see the child development charts that start on page 229.

Try to become aware of your attitude toward your deaf child's ability. Do you expect him to do less than he is actually capable of?

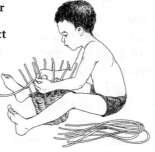

CHILDREN LEARN SOCIAL SKILLS IN STEPS

Like all kinds of development, children learn social skills in steps. To develop social skills, a child needs to become aware of other people's feelings. And she needs to learn how to share and cooperate with other people.

At first a child plays alongside other children. This means she enjoys being near them as she plays, but she does not actually play with them.

Then she learns to play with others. She learns to share toys and play games where everyone must cooperate.

As children get older, they need to understand rules and be able to control their behavior.

Even though Callam wants a sweet, he has learned not to grab it out of another child's hand.

AT HOME

Children first learn social skills by watching how parents and family members behave with each other. Children copy what others do and what they say as they interact with each other.

Please have a little soup, Haseeb.

Can I have some too, please!

Me next?

PLAYING WITH OTHER CHILDREN

As they play, children learn to follow directions, cooperate, take turns, and share. Play helps young children understand their own emotions, feel proud of what they can do, and develop a sense of who they are.

IN THE COMMUNITY

Outside their own homes and immediate families, children see how older children and adults talk, play, and work with each other. This is how children learn ways to relate to people outside their families. And in the wider world that opens to them, children learn to practice different responses to situations and different ways of doing things. They develop social skills as they discover their own strengths and weaknesses.

I am glad to have your help keeping bugs off the bean plants.

Mr. Lopes, which bugs are the bad ones?

Deafness makes it harder to learn social skills

Children who can hear learn a lot about the world by listening to what goes on around them. Many of the social skills they learn are never taught to them directly, but develop as they listen to other people talking with each other. Children who cannot hear miss a lot of this information.

Ramani! Put that back — it's not yours!

Oh, that's fine, she can have it.

No, she should know better!

A child who cannot hear well often finds it harder than other children to learn how to behave with other people. She does not understand the behavior she sees and the reasons why people behave a certain way.

Ramani wants a banana, but she doesn't understand that her mother must pay for it first.

This is true especially when a deaf child and her parents are not able to communicate well with each other. When she misbehaves it may be difficult to explain how she should act. She may become frustrated and misbehave even more. A child who misbehaves a lot may get left alone by other people.

A deaf child needs extra help learning how to communicate, how to cooperate with others, and how to control her behavior.

How to manage your child's behavior

Deafness does not cause bad behavior, though it may seem like it does. A child who cannot hear well communicates mainly through his behavior — just like a hearing child whose communication skills have not yet developed.

Learn to recognize the signals that tell you problem behavior is about to begin.

We have to go home right now, Paulo.

Paulo looks surprised and unhappy. He may start to yell and cry soon.

If Paulo could hear, he would have heard his mother and grandmother talking and known they were leaving soon.

He would have been better prepared for what would happen next.

Since Paulo cannot hear well, he is surprised when his grandmother tells him they have to go home. Like Paulo, deaf children experience surprises all the time.

Parents need to pay close attention to how a child who is deaf or cannot hear well is behaving. It takes patience to understand what your child is communicating to you with his behavior and learn how to communicate your expectations.

Children who can hear learn good behavior more easily, and at a younger age, than children who cannot hear. Children may go through times when they say 'no' to everything a parent wants them to do. These behaviors can be very frustrating to a child's family, but they are normal and usually go away when a child learns better self-control.

It is much more difficult for a child who cannot hear well to learn self-control. When people cannot communicate with deaf children, the children become frustrated, upset, or angry. They cannot understand why they must do certain things or what is happening around them.

Aaaah!

TRY TO PREVENT PROBLEMS FROM STARTING

When your child behaves badly, ask yourself, 'What is my child trying to tell me?', 'What does she need?'. Remember that your child's behavior is one of the ways she communicates with you. Because she cannot communicate in words or signs, she is often telling you something with her behavior.

You may be able to avoid certain behavior problems if you understand what causes them. Your child may:

- need attention. She may have learned that she gets more attention if she behaves badly.

- feel tired, hungry, or afraid of something.

- not understand what you want. Or she may want something but be unable to communicate it so you understand.

- have been teased or treated badly by another child or adult.

- be copying another child's behavior.

- not be able to meet your expectations. Or she may be resisting limits that you have set, or showing you she does not want to do what you want.

Even though you may understand why your child becomes upset, there will be times when she gets upset no matter what you do. But if you can see a child's behavior as her way of communicating with you, you may be able to take care of the child's need before it becomes a problem.

HOW TO SET LIMITS

Even when your child behaves well, there are times when you have to tell your child 'no', and set limits on the child's behavior. This may be to keep your child safe, or because he is misbehaving, or because he wants to do something you cannot allow him to do. Children of different ages need to have different limits. The limits you set will change as your child gets older and learns more about the world.

Because your child cannot hear well, sometimes she will not understand what you want. When you say 'no', or you tell your child what you want her to do, you may not have enough communication skills to make her understand. You may think your child is ignoring you or misbehaving, when in fact she does not understand what you want or do not want her to do.

Anita does not understand what her father is telling her.

When you want to limit the child's behavior or change what the child is doing:

1. **Tell** him. Before you say 'no', think about it carefully. When you

No, you must stay here.

say 'no' you should be firm about it. If you let your child change your mind by his bad behavior, then he will learn to misbehave in order to get what he wants.

Once you tell your child that he cannot do something or have something, you should not change your mind just to stop his crying.

2. **Show** him what you mean.

These are Papa's eyeglasses, Sunil. They are not for playing with!

3. **Use pictures** to make the request clearer.

You must cover the well or someone could fall in!

Pictures are especially helpful for things that are hard to communicate — like how a child´s actions affect others.

4. **Help** him do as you request.

If the deaf child has trouble understanding what you requested, show him by doing what you mean.

WAYS TO MANAGE BEHAVIOR THAT **DO NOT** WORK WELL

Families with deaf children may be faced with behavior problems they do not know how to handle. They sometimes use solutions that work for them at the moment — even if those ways do not help the child learn good behavior. Here are some examples of things that do not work well:

- Using commands without explaining the reasons for them or what they mean. This prevents the child from making good decisions by himself.

- Punishing a child who is deaf more than other children. Physical abuse can make a child depressed and violent.

- Allowing the misbehavior of a child who cannot hear well to continue without correcting it. This makes the child more socially isolated.

- Keeping a child who cannot hear well at home more than other children. This holds back the child's social development.

While these methods may seem to work for the moment, they will not help a child learn how to behave well or interact with other people.

All parents want their children to behave well and grow up to be accepted members of the community. For your child to develop self-control, your own self-control can be a model. Show your child the kind of behavior that makes anyone a good person to live with.

▶ How to help your child calm down when he behaves badly

When your child is behaving badly, take him to a different spot and make him sit for about 5 minutes (less time for a very young child). If he tries to leave before the time is up, start the time over again. Do not leave him alone. You can use a 'time out' like this to give your child a chance to think about his behavior and how he can do better. 'Time outs' also give you time to calm down when you are frustrated and upset.

Before giving him a 'time out', hold him firmly and explain to him how you want him to behave. When he is calmer, communicate with him about why he needed a 'time out' and about how his behavior affects others. Always remind him that you like him, but that you do not like the way he acted. Encourage him to talk or sign about what happened and why and how he could react differently. Help him understand why he needed the 'time out'.

Omar, kicking your brother is wrong. Let's think of another way you can let him know when you are angry.

What to do if your child has a tantrum

As with many other young children, your child's anger may become a 'temper tantrum'. A tantrum is when a child completely loses control and screams, kicks, hits, or cries. Children who cannot communicate easily usually have more tantrums than other children, and it may be harder to calm them down.

It is important for you stay as calm as you can. Take a minute to decide what to do. Here are some useful ways to deal with tantrums:

- Do not try to explain things to him once he has lost control. This is not the time for a discussion.

- Do not respond to your child's screaming and kicking, but do not leave him completely alone. His behavior may frighten him and he needs you nearby for security.

- Do not spank, pinch, shake, or scream at your child. This will only make the tantrum worse. But do not let him hit you. You can hold him, but only to prevent him from hurting himself, hurting you, or breaking things.

- Try to distract a child during a tantrum. For example, if your child yells because you have taken something away from him, you can try to offer something else that he wants or show him something unusual. This works better with very young children.

Take a child who is having a tantrum away from the situation if you can.

If the tantrum is in response to a limit you have set, do not allow your child's behavior to change the limit. If you give in to your child's behavior, he will learn that he can get what he wants from you by having a tantrum.

When your child misbehaves or has a tantrum in public

If a child behaves badly in public, pick the child up if you can and remove her from the situation. Try to act calmly and without anger. Take her out of the store, away from the market, or wherever the problem happens. If you can, find a private place for her to calm down. If neccessary, have someone else stay with her while you finish what you need to do.

It may seem easier to keep a child at home than to worry about behavior problems in public. But it is important for all children to learn how to behave in public and to be part of the community.

OUR ACTIONS ARE POWERFUL TEACHERS

As with any family, it is very important for a family with a deaf child to set a good example. The family must act the way they want their deaf child to act, and encourage their child by explaining what kind of behavior they like. But it is not easy to set a good example and encourage children to behave well.

Raising small children can often be frustrating. And when communication is difficult, it is even harder to teach a child how to behave. Because communication with deaf children is more difficult, parents and other caregivers may become frustrated with them and hit or shake them more than hearing children. See Chapter 17 for more information to help parents and caregivers.

No, Oscar!

It can be hard for people to change the ways they discipline children. Most people discipline children the same way they themselves were disciplined as children. But when we handle our own frustration without becoming violent, we are sending our children a powerful message that they too can handle frustration without violence. Here is a story about how one group of parents worked to change the way they disciplined their children.

Parents in Mexico find another way to discipline

In Oaxaca, Mexico, a preschool program for deaf children was started by a social worker and a teacher. Every day parents came to the program with their children. The parents participated in the activities with their children and they supported each other.

After a while, the parents began to notice how often they hit or shook their deaf children. They talked it over with the social worker and decided they wanted to find another way to discipline their children. The social worker explained the idea of a 'time out': taking the child away from the problem situation and having the child sit quietly for a few minutes.

The parents decided it would help them to stop hitting their children if they fined themselves a few pesos every time they hit or shook their child. They put an empty tin can on a shelf to hold the money. At first, almost every parent was putting money in the tin can every day. But the fines helped them to stop and think before they hit or shook their children.

Maria always grabs things from her sisters. They let her do it because she is little. But she is getting bigger and she should know better.

Hugo used to do that. I found myself hitting him a lot, but I couldn't explain why it was wrong. I used to feel angry and sad at the same time.

It is getting better as we learn to communicate. But it takes so long to learn! I try hard not to get angry.

As they tried new methods and improved their communication skills, they noticed that their children were behaving better. At the beginning, it did not seem easy to change how they disciplined their children, but now they almost never hit or shake them.

How to encourage a child's social development

Help your child get to know adults who are deaf or cannot hear well.

This helps her learn that adults who cannot hear can still be successful, and will help her build confidence and self-esteem. If she sees them cooperating, asking questions, responding and expressing feelings, she will learn social rules and develop her social skills.

I always wanted to be just like my big sister.

Me too!

How many brothers and sisters do you have?

Encourage your child to become responsible and independent.

Good job, Kofi. You did it yourself!

Help him be aware of skills he already has that are valued or useful in the community. Encourage him to develop these skills even more.

Fatuma says I am a big help to Mama. I can get wood for Grandma too.

HELP A CHILD COMMUNICATE ABOUT HIS FEELINGS

A child who cannot talk about his feelings may have no choice but to act them out instead. He may hit, scream, or kick when he is frustrated or angry because he has no other way to express those feelings. If your child is often frustrated, rude, or angry, you need to help him learn to express his feelings in other ways.

Look for opportunities to teach your child signs and words for strong emotions. This will help him know and understand his emotions. When he does, he will find it easier to talk or sign about his emotions rather than acting them out.

> *Those men are very angry, Moshe. Sometimes you feel angry too. Like when Aminata broke your toy.*

REWARD GOOD BEHAVIOR

When a child behaves well, he is treated well by the people around him. When your child is behaving well, praise him. A child wants the love and approval of his parents and others, and he will repeat the behavior that brings praise and attention. A few comments during the day, or giving him a hug or a treat, will go a long way to encourage good behavior.

Teaching a deaf child good behavior takes patience and hard work. But once he begins to develop social skills and behaves well, it will be easier for him to make friends, join the community, and eventually go to school.

- Praise her when she does something well.

> *Good job, Sisi!*

Mother encourages Sisi when she tries to wash her clothes.

- Reward good behavior rather than problem behavior. Give your child a smile or a loving pat when you like the way he is behaving.

Often a child continues a problem behavior because he has learned that it will get him what he wants. For example:

Kwame has been left to play by himself. He tries to get his mother to come play with him.

When she does not, Kwame starts yelling. His mother comes to see what's wrong.

Now Kwame has her full attention.

Refusing attention when Kwame is being nice...   and giving it only when he begins to yell...   encourages bad behavior.

But if you give your child attention when he behaves well and refuse it when he behaves badly, you can teach him that acting badly does not get him what he wants. For example, Kwame's mother learned that:

Giving attention when Kwame is being nice...   but refusing it when he yells...   encourages good behavior.

LET A CHILD KNOW 'WHY'

It is easier for children to do something you ask if they know **why**
they should do it. But because young
children who cannot hear well may
not know enough words or signs to
understand 'why', parents often
find it easier just to tell them
what to do. If children do
not understand why they
have to do something,
they can become
frustrated.

Hoa, I said stop
playing and
hurry up!

Hoa might walk
more quickly if his
father could
explain to him that
dinner is waiting
for them at home!

MAKE CHANGE EASIER

Transitions (changing from one activity to another) can be difficult
for many young children. They may get upset at going from one
house to another, or at having to stop playing in order to take a
bath. They still have to get used to daily routines. Until they learn to
expect a chain of daily activities and become comfortable with this,
children may struggle with the ordinary routines of the day. And
when they get used to a routine, even small changes can make
children feel insecure.

It is easier for children to
accept changes when they
know what to expect. Pictures
can sometimes help you
communicate about
transitions. For example, if
your child is playing and it is
time for his bath, you can
show a picture of him taking
a bath. Discussing what the

Julio, it is bath
time. I am
heating the
water now.

picture communicates can give him a chance to prepare for the
change and may make the transition easier for both of you.

To make going out in public easier, it may help if you explain to your
child where you are going before you go. For example, show him
your basket to help him understand you are going to the market.

Remember — change will be easier as children get older.

Help your child learn to make decisions

One of the most important things children need to learn is how to make good decisions. If you or others tell a child what to do all the time, she will not learn to make good decisions.

Being able to make good decisions helps children become confident. Being confident will help them participate fully in the activities of their communities and help them have better lives. Whenever you can, encourage your child to make simple choices about things that affect her. For example, sometimes she can decide what to eat or drink, what to wear, when to sleep, or choose what to do.

Let's see if Pu Yi understands that she can choose either a round bun or a long bun.

If a deaf child wants to make a decision but cannot tell you what she wants or likes, try asking her questions to help her communicate what she would like to do.

Everyone can help deaf children develop social skills

Children who are deaf can learn and practice their social skills best when they are part of a caring community, and when they go to school. When children interact and spend time in a social group outside the family, they make a big leap in developing their social skills. Some communities have child care centers or preschools, where groups of children can play and learn together. The children understand that expectations are different in a group setting. They learn to share, take turns, and think about the feelings of others.

Help a deaf child learn about the world

It is important for children who are deaf or cannot hear well to experience community events, take part in daily activities and discuss these with their families and friends. Parents, sisters, and brothers can help by taking a deaf child out as much as possible to public places and to visit relatives and friends. You can use every chance to teach the child how things work in the community.

Take her with you when you collect water, gather wood, or when you go to the market, to school, to places of worship, to festivals, or to community meetings and events. Along the way, try to notice what hearing children can learn just by listening. Try to explain these things to your child by using signs or words that you both understand.

For this money you can have 2.

By watching others, children can learn about the world around them. They can learn things like who grows the food they eat, and how people buy and sell at the market.

HELP YOUR CHILD DEVELOP FRIENDSHIPS

As children begin playing more with each other, communication and the ability to get along with others become more important. Many deaf children are lonely and isolated. This is partly because they have not learned enough social skills to develop friendships. It is also because hearing children do not know how to include them.

Since Rina can't hear well, let's play a game where hearing doesn't matter!

We could use hand signals instead of saying words for 'ready', and 'out'.

You can help children in the community who are not deaf understand how to communicate with deaf children. When other children know how to communicate with a deaf child, they may be more willing to include her in their games.

Children often make up games of 'pretend'. If they include a deaf child, it can help him learn about what to expect in new situations and how to behave.

Simon's brother and sister are playing 'store' to help him understand how people act in stores and how things are purchased.

To help your child make friends and play with other children, help her become aware of other people's feelings, learn to share and cooperate, and understand rules. She may also need help communicating with other children.

Other children may become frustrated trying to play with a child who does not understand the rules of their game. They may start to leave the deaf child out of their games. You can help by showing hearing children ways to play that do not need words. You can explain the rules to your child and show her how to play the game.

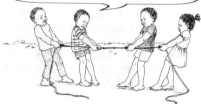

Rina is so strong! I want her on my team next time.

The 'social skills' of the community

While teaching social skills to children is very important, that alone is not enough. Children learn social skills not only from how we teach them and treat them, but also from how they see people treating each other in their community.

When we teach children to be friends with children who are deaf, and to respect those who are different, we are helping them understand that we value compassion. We are teaching them that helping others is **everyone's** responsibility.

When we teach children to play together in a group, we are helping them understand that we value solidarity and cooperation.

But we must take our own advice, and set an example by our own actions! If our children see us ignoring or rejecting those who have different abilities from ourselves, or those who look different, or who are poor, they will learn a very different lesson from what we mean to teach them.

When we are kind and respectful to others, children learn that this is how people should treat each other.

If we want our children to learn to respect themselves and others, they must see us putting these values into practice. We ourselves must show respect for people who are different. All of us must also work to create a community that welcomes and supports all people, and acts on the values that are important to us.

Chapter 11
Working together to help children who are deaf

There are many ways that communities can work together to make a difference for their deaf children. They can make the community a better place for children who are deaf by raising awareness about the needs and capabilities of people who are deaf or cannot hear well. Communities can support families with children who cannot hear well and they can make it possible for deaf children to get an education.

What is your community?

The main community that most people consider their own is their neighborhood, or the area where they live. But there are many other kinds of community. Many groups can provide support for deaf children and their families since families with deaf children often belong to many different communities at the same time.

families with deaf children

the school

deaf people in your country

the village

deaf people everywhere

CHILDREN WHO LEARN AND PLAY TOGETHER FORM A COMMUNITY

Children are a natural community for each other. But children need encouragement to include others who are different from them — whether they are deaf or have some other difference. Adults and older children can help children learn to respect others and to develop qualities like patience, fairness, and caring. For more information about how to encourage children with different hearing abilities to relate to each other, see Chapter 10 on developing social skills.

DEAF PEOPLE FORM A COMMUNITY

Sometimes, people who are deaf may feel there is no community that cares about their welfare. In many communities, people who are deaf or cannot hear well are made to feel unwelcome by their families, relatives, neighbors and others who do not know how to communicate with them. Sometimes other people laugh at them and tease them. And it can be especially hard for parents of a deaf child to see their child getting teased by other people. Wherever they are, people who are deaf or cannot hear well often face similar problems. Many deaf people still have few opportunities to take their place within society.

Deaf people often feel a close bond with each other because they face similar problems and share a similar way of communicating, like sign language. Whether they live nearby or must travel to visit each other, deaf people play a very important part in each other's lives.

Anywhere there are 2 or more deaf people together, there is a community — created by the common experience of being deaf.

Oh, I know. Me too!

People who are deaf can be a source of comfort and guidance to each other. When they can meet together they usually form very strong communities. Communities may form around deaf schools, as deaf children learn and grow up together. Or deaf people may gather in deaf clubs, work cooperatives or religious organizations.

Deaf adults can also be a great help to families that are raising deaf children, because they understand the needs and challenges these families often face.

HEARING PEOPLE WHO WELCOME DEAF PEOPLE CAN HELP BRING COMMUNITIES TOGETHER

Many hearing people realize the value of friendship with deaf people. They may have deaf friends, work with a deaf person, or they may have family members who cannot hear well. Hearing people who are comfortable communicating with deaf people can build bridges between the hearing and deaf communities. When hearing people learn sign language, they can help deaf and hearing people understand each other and help deaf children thrive.

Joseph and the deaf choir

Joseph, a young man from Haiti who can hear, learned sign language at a class in his neighborhood. Joseph made friends with some of the deaf people in his city. They encouraged him to volunteer at a church that held prayer services for deaf people. Joseph learned to translate the prayers from spoken language to sign language.

As he got more involved, he began teaching young deaf people at the church to sign (and sing out loud) some of the songs that were used in the prayer service. Soon a whole choir of young deaf people was singing and signing with him.

Now Joseph and the deaf choir drive far into the rural mountains of Haiti where they sing at other churches. Many people approach Joseph to ask him about the choir, and tell him about the deaf children in their own families.

Joseph uses the opportunity to tell people about a program for young deaf children in one of the towns, and about the residential school for older deaf children in his city.

By bringing young deaf people to rural churches, Joseph has been able to bring the hearing community and the deaf community closer together.

Making the community a better place for children who are deaf

RAISING AWARENESS

The way that adults and older children act towards deaf children can have a strong effect on others. For example, if people include deaf children in their activities, or if they oppose poor treatment of deaf children, it is more likely that others will follow their example. Here is a story about a school principal in Mongolia who used his position to influence how deaf children were treated in his school.

A school learns to welcome deaf children

In one town in Mongolia, a few families worked hard to organize classes for deaf children in their local school. After some cases of teasing and making fun of the deaf children, the school principal called all the students to a meeting and explained to them that this behavior was not acceptable, and that all children at the school should feel welcome.

Everyone's behavior changed when the school principal insisted on better treatment of the children who could not hear. As time passed, the teachers, parents, and students began to feel proud of their deaf classes and feel responsible for the students. Now, when the other children meet their deaf schoolmates outside the school, they are friendly to them. Children from other classes often visit the deaf class, and some of the older girls have taught the young deaf children the complicated steps of traditional Mongolian dances.

Come play ball with us.

Okay!

Help people communicate with your child

Adults and children in the community can help deaf children by interacting with them. They must treat deaf children with the same respect and kindness they show to others. When community members communicate with deaf children, they will learn that children who are deaf are just like other children.

Encourage people to communicate with your child whenever they see her. Introduce her to people you meet. Show them how to greet her, and teach her how to greet them. Just as you teach a hearing child the name or term of respect for each person you know in the community, teach your child a sign or spoken name for each person, and teach people your child's sign or spoken name.

People in the community may feel more comfortable with your child if you explain how to act, and show them a few signs or gestures. Explain to people that it is best to be at the same eye level as your child when they talk or sign to her. People can use gestures and expressions on their faces as if they are communicating with a child who can hear.

Good morning, Alicia.

Families of deaf children can organize programs for people in the neighborhood to help them understand about 'differences', respect, and awareness of deafness and hearing. They can help their friends and community-based groups to welcome children who are deaf or 'different' in other ways.

People will better understand a child who does not hear well if they can get an idea of what that might feel like. Here are some fun ways to learn. These games can be used in public places such as churches, temples or other religious places, clinics, schools, and community groups. You can use them during awareness-raising sessions or during a parents' meeting.

▶ How to help hearing people understand what it is like to be deaf or not hear well

Game: What did you say?

One person covers his ears while another tells a funny story to the group. Or people can take turns sitting far away, so they cannot hear the story. Another person asks everyone questions about the story, including the person whose ears were covered or who sat far away.

Ask this person what it felt like not being able to hear the story well.

Then everyone can talk about what they can do to communicate better with children who really do have difficulty hearing.

▶ How to help children communicate without speech

Children who have difficulty hearing usually have difficulty speaking. Their speech sounds strange to people who can hear. This is because people who cannot hear have no way to know how speech is supposed to sound. It is very hard for them to speak like hearing people do. As a result, many deaf people choose not to speak, and communicate only with gestures, or signs or sign language. People with different hearing abilities may feel shy and only talk to the people they know well.

Ask a group of children if they know other children in the community who are deaf or cannot hear well. You can all discuss ways to communicate with children who have different hearing abilities.

Game: Talking without words

This game will help children understand how difficult it can be for a child who cannot speak, or who cannot speak well, to communicate. Everyone takes turns trying to say something to the group without using words. Begin with easy ideas, like 'I am sleepy', or 'give me the ball'. Then try harder ones, like 'I'm lost and can't find my house', or 'I had a bad dream'.

Afterwards, you can talk about:

- Was it difficult to explain something without talking?

- How did you feel when someone did not understand?

- What did other children do that helped you communicate with them? What else could they have done to help?

- How might you communicate with children who cannot speak?

Then you could make up some signs for the ideas you tried. See how much easier it is to communicate with signs.

This is a good time to tell children about their local sign language or about how families can make up signs to help each other communicate (see Chapter 4). To help children learn some home signs, see pages 40 to 43 in Chapter 4.

SERVICES FOR DEAF CHILDREN AND THEIR FAMILIES

All people need basic services such as water, electricity, transportation, education, and health care. It usually takes the resources of a whole community to provide services like these. The same is true of services needed by deaf children and their families. People in the community have knowledge, resources, and skills they can share. By working together, a group of families or an entire community can organize efforts toward things like:

- learning how to check the hearing of young children.

- helping local health workers learn to recognize and treat ear infections, which can help prevent deafness.

A safety sign like this can make a street safer for everyone!

- finding a place where families with deaf children can meet.

- organizing speech or sign language classes.

- helping hearing people learn to talk so that children who can hear a little can understand them.

- translating between sign and speech at schools or play groups.

One group of parents in India worked to bring hearing aid services to their town, so that children would have trained health workers nearby to fit, repair, and maintain their hearing aids.

A parents' group or village health association can invite organizations or people from outside the community to visit the village to start new services, give training, or lead discussions. Or the community can collect money to send one person for training. This person can then train others when she returns.

Form support groups

Families of deaf children are important resources for each other. By organizing regular meetings, they can help each other with problems they face, and share suggestions of new ideas and opportunities for their children. This can be a great help, not only in organizing for their children's needs, but also in giving each other support as they overcome challenges.

The community can help this happen by providing space for meetings (for example, at a local temple, church, or mosque) and by letting people know about the meetings, so that other families can join.

Families with deaf children face many similar challenges and experience similar joys. See Chapter 14 for examples of how parents can start a group where they share feelings, information, and ideas to make a community more supportive for their children.

OTHER COMMUNITY ORGANIZATIONS CAN GIVE SUPPORT

Many local community-based groups such as women's groups, parents' groups, farmers' groups, or credit or income generation groups can provide support to parents of children who have difficulty hearing.

For example, families may need extra time to teach and look after a child who cannot hear well. This might make it difficult to find paid work outside the home. A community-based group could help parents find ways to earn an income. Community-based groups such as a mother's group can also help deaf children get hearing aids, find resources to pay sign language teachers, arrange opportunities for early childhood education, subsidize payment of school fees, or help in other ways.

BRING DEAF CHILDREN TOGETHER WITH OTHER DEAF PEOPLE

A community's efforts to support deaf children can also bring them together. When children who are deaf or cannot hear well have an opportunity to meet together they can begin to form a natural community and develop their language and communication skills.

One town in China took a survey to find out how many deaf children there were who might attend a deaf school. Because of this survey, two families living next to each other were surprised to find that they both had deaf family members who had never met!

If you live in a large town or city, you can probably find ways to meet other deaf people. Even if you live in a small village there may be some deaf and hearing people who communicate using signs and gestures. They will often be happy to help families with deaf children.

Are you coming to eat at our house tonight? Ravi and Mita will be there too!

Many larger communities have social clubs, associations, or large informal groups made up of people who are deaf. Sometimes these associations have programs for deaf children and their families. You and your child will be welcome there.

Deaf people who communicate well are often the best teachers and advisors for a family with a deaf child.

Every year the Delhi Foundation of Deaf Women, in India, has a talent contest for deaf children. After the contest, families meet and learn about deafness. This is part of the foundation's 'Catch Them Young' program to involve families with young deaf children in deaf community activities.

HELP DEAF CHILDREN GET EDUCATION AND TRAINING

Many families struggle to give their children who cannot hear well the chance to go to school. It takes time, energy, and resources to organize opportunities for deaf children to learn. But when a whole community works for educational rights for deaf children, it can make a big difference.

Chapter 12 describes in more detail the benefits that different kinds of schools or classes may have for deaf children and their families.

Communities interested in organizing better education and training for deaf children should contact their local or national association for the deaf, and the Ministry of Education. This will help them learn more about the opportunities and laws about deaf education in the area. The laws of most countries support the rights of all children — including deaf children — to a public education.

Awareness is the first step towards change

Deaf adults, parents, and community members must work with government officials so that the officials know the needs of deaf children and what deaf children can be capable of. Together they can dispel the ignorance and the myths that surround deafness.

*If the president or the prime minister had a child who could not hear well, **then** there would be schools and teachers for our children!*

Here are some ways a community can help schools meet deaf children's needs better:

- Offer extra training to teachers so they can learn how to communicate with deaf children.

- Invite deaf adults to help teachers, families, or students learn sign language. Or they can work in the classroom and give extra attention to the deaf students. Chapter 12 includes more activities that help deaf children learn in local schools.

- Offer extra training in skills that will help students earn an income.

Bringing deaf children together in their own school or classroom can create a community of children who might otherwise have been isolated from each other. Some communities get money from local or national associations, donor organizations, or their government to help pay for training and facilities.

EVERYONE BENEFITS FROM EFFORTS TO SUPPORT DEAF CHILDREN

The entire community becomes stronger when people take care of each other, are responsible for each other, and when they accept

people's differences as well as the things they have in common. So when attention is given to the special needs of deaf children, it often improves conditions for the entire community.

All children in the community can benefit from improved social services like hearing tests and better access to education and training.

When people learn to work together toward a common goal they learn that they can achieve much more together than alone. A community that organizes around one issue will be able to use that experience to address other needs and do other projects.

When teachers find ways to communicate with children who cannot hear, it can help all children to understand their lessons better.

Aren't you afraid that having those deaf children in your class will slow the class down?

No, I think the other children need to learn some patience! And all of their reading is getting stronger. They are also learning sign language.

If children who cannot hear well do not get education and support, they may never learn to communicate with other people or learn useful skills to get work, take care of themselves, or live peacefully with others. Their unhappiness and poverty may become a burden on their families, neighborhoods, and communities.

Here is a story about how a group in Brazil is working in their community to change the lives of deaf children.

A town learns a new language

In a northeastern town in Brazil, a church started a small school for deaf children. Soon the families that attended began a parents group, the Association of Parents and Friends of the Deaf in Cabo (APASC). As a group, APASC decided to offer sign language classes to hearing people so that they could communicate with their deaf children. They contacted the deaf association in the neighboring big city and hired a deaf man to teach the parents and their family members sign language.

More and more people took sign language classes and learned how to communicate with the deaf children and deaf adults who lived in the town.

APASC also got the local government to open the local school to their deaf children. The school hired trained teachers and started classes for deaf children. The deaf children joined the hearing children in many of the school's activities. Soon, the town was seeing sign language in the schools, in the shops, and in the streets.

Before, many people had thought that deaf people were mentally slow. Now, they have new ideas about deafness. They see sign language interpreters at church services, deaf teenagers getting jobs in the community, and deaf children studying and playing with hearing children.

APASC helped raise the level of awareness about deafness in their community. They have workshops and monthly meetings where parents can find support from other parents, and learn about deafness and how to communicate with their deaf children. APASC also printed a simple sign language dictionary with 500 signs that many people in the community use.

By working together, they are building a society that helps all children develop to their full potential.

Chapter 12

Education

All children — deaf and hearing — have a right to education. Children who get an education have more opportunities to learn about the world, develop skills, and find jobs. Education is especially important for deaf children because it allows them to develop their thinking, to communicate with other deaf and hearing people, and to make friends. And with the skills they gain, children who cannot hear well will be able to live productive, independent lives and take part in the life of the community.

Though this book is mostly for children from birth to age 5, this chapter includes some important issues about educating older deaf children, to help parents plan for their child's education.

Learning begins at home

Learning begins at home, in a child's infancy, and continues throughout her life. The family plays a very important role in helping children learn. Parents and family members are the earliest and most important teachers. At home, a child will learn to communicate, start thinking, and begin relating to other people.

Some communities have teachers and deaf adults who come to peoples' homes to help parents learn how to communicate with their deaf child. They show family members activities they can do together to learn language. (For ideas and activities to help families teach their children a language, see Chapters 7, 8, and 9.)

Learning continues in the community

Children learn from their families and friends the skills they need to live in their community. By watching how children and other people talk, play, and work with each other, children learn how to get along with others. They learn to get places they need to go — walking, riding, or driving. They learn to buy and sell, to pay bills, and to get things done. They learn to gather wood, plant crops, fish, weave or sew, make handcrafts, and many other skills.

With this money we will buy some fish at the market.

Education takes place in many situations: at home, in the community, and at school.

When children participate in the community, they also learn about their emotions and build self-esteem. Games they play with each other are informal ways of learning to be part of communities. (Chapter 10 and Chapter 11 describe ways to include children in the community and to build strong social skills.)

As children grow older they become ready to go to school. Education in school will build on the skills children learn at home and in the community. What they learn at school also gives children skills that prepare them for life as adults.

Going to school is important for deaf children

Education in school will improve the ability of children who are deaf or cannot hear well to communicate, and can give them skills to lead productive lives and to support their families.

I'm going to write a letter to my brother who went away to work in the city.

At school, deaf children can learn to read and write — often the only ways that deaf people can communicate with people who do not know sign language or cannot understand their speech. Reading helps people who cannot hear well understand the ideas, emotions, and experiences of other people. Writing helps them communicate and share their thoughts and emotions.

Deaf girls especially need education!

It is often even more difficult for a deaf girl to get an education. A girl who cannot hear well is often kept at home doing housework — even after her sisters and brothers leave to go to school or get married.

> *You don't have to worry about Chung-Yi. You did the right thing by sending her to school. One day she will be able to look after you!*

Why does a deaf girl need to know about the world? She needs skills to keep herself safe and take part in her community. She needs to know her rights, and get the skills to have a job and live an independent life.

Without communication and education, a deaf girl cannot learn about social rules or understand changes in her body. Too many deaf girls become pregnant without knowing how or why. In some parts of the world, more deaf women have HIV/AIDS than other women because they do not have a way to get the information they need to stay safe.

Different kinds of schools for deaf children

Children who are deaf or cannot hear well can go to school and learn a lot, including skills they will need to earn a living. They can learn in regular classes together with hearing children, or separately with other deaf children.

> *Pama will be old enough for school next year, but I don't know what school will be best for her.*

> *My sister's son goes to a residential school for deaf children. The next time she visits, you must come and ask her about it.*

> *Or maybe Pama can go to our neighborhood school. She has a right to go there like any other child!*

> *We would have to help make sure that the teacher knows how to teach a deaf child.*

Even though you may not have many choices about the kind of school to send your child to, knowing about schools is important because:

- it can help you think about what would be best for your child.

- it can help you work with your school to make the school better for deaf children.

- it can help you work with the community to get the kind of school that families with deaf children need.

Schools and language

Schools that teach deaf children usually focus either on the **spoken language** of the community or on **sign language**. Some schools teach deaf children to speak and use sign language at the same time, or to speak and use finger spelling. They use sign language, gestures, pictures, lip reading, speech, and reading and writing.

Often the teachers who use spoken language and teachers who use sign language do not agree with each other's methods. This can make it very difficult for parents to get information about what is good in each method.

Our school believes that deaf children have a right to learn sign language, as it is the 'natural language' for deaf people.

Our school believes that only deaf children who can understand and respond to spoken language can succeed in the world.

We also teach about the history and importance of deaf people and the deaf community.

See Chapters 7 to 9 for information about spoken and sign languages and how to start using them. It is important to remember that each child has his or her own needs and abilities.

DEAF CHILDREN CAN LEARN IN THE SAME CLASSES AS HEARING CHILDREN

Teaching deaf children and hearing children in the same class is often the only way a community is able to educate deaf children. Children who hear may tease or ignore deaf children because of the way they speak or because they may not understand what people say. But if people make an effort to stop that kind of hurtful behavior, deaf children can have the opportunity to make friends with hearing children and to become part of the local community.

We deaf and hearing children would not want to be separated — we would be losing our good friends!

*We help those who can't hear **see** what they need to know.*

We push those in their wheelchairs if they need help.

We lend each other things we have forgotten.

As the children become part of each other's lives, they learn to appreciate each other's strengths and support each other.

Some local schools teach everyone sign language so deaf children are not left out. Or they spend extra time to teach children who cannot hear well to speak.

Benefits of learning with hearing children

- Deaf children can continue living at home with their families.
- It is often less expensive.

Difficulties of learning with hearing children

- Children who can hear may tease or ignore deaf children.
- Teachers may not be able to learn much about deafness or how to teach children with different hearing abilities.
- There may not be enough people fluent in sign language to learn a complete language. The child's mental development may suffer.

▶ *Ways to support deaf children in hearing classrooms*

It is not enough just to open the school doors to deaf children. A deaf child who learns in a regular classroom needs a teacher and classmates who can communicate with her. Lessons must be taught in a way deaf children can understand. If a deaf child cannot understand, she will not learn.

When schools do not provide enough support for deaf children, they will not learn as well as hearing children. If schools expect deaf children to learn less, then all children will learn the same thing — deaf children are less capable. This idea is not true and harms everyone.

Offer extra training to teachers so they can learn how to communicate with deaf children

A teacher who has not worked with children who are deaf or who can hear only a little may be unsure about how to teach a child who does not hear well. Talk to the teacher about the child's needs and abilities, and see if there are simple ways to make learning easier for the child.

If a child can hear a little or read lips, the teacher should face the child when she speaks and check often to make sure the child can see her mouth.

Let the child sit close to the teacher. She will be better able to see the teacher's lips move. She will also be less distracted by the movements of other children.

Help schools meet a deaf child's needs:

- Teachers can prepare the rest of the school — the other teachers and children — about deafness and about how deaf children learn best by seeing. This way everyone in the school can get ready to welcome deaf children.

- Deaf adults can help the teacher or the students learn sign language. They can help the teacher in the classroom by giving extra attention to the deaf students.

- Because children who are deaf or cannot hear well learn by seeing, schools can help them have their eyes checked and get glasses, if needed.

Parents can meet with a child's teachers to get information about what and how she is learning. This will help parents strengthen and build on what their child is learning at school. They can also tell the teacher about what the child does at home. That way the teacher can include things from the child's experience in her lessons.

DEAF CHILDREN CAN LEARN IN THEIR OWN GROUP

Children who are deaf or cannot hear well can learn in separate classrooms for deaf children in a local school, or in separate day schools or residential schools.

Many local or national associations, or government, religious, community, or aid organizations have started separate schools or classrooms to educate children who are deaf or cannot hear well. These organizations may even offer scholarships for children who are deaf or do not hear well to study in such schools or classrooms. Bringing deaf children together in their own schools or classrooms creates a community of children who otherwise might have been isolated from each other.

When children attend schools like these, they often learn sign language. Family members will be able to communicate better with their children if they learn sign language too.

Residential schools

Deaf children live at these schools and return home only for weekends or holidays. Children at residential schools often learn skills for work, like computers, mechanics, art, and farming, as well as reading, writing, and math.

Families sometimes worry about their children when they are far from home. Communicating with families of other students, visiting their children at school, and meeting the children's friends and teachers can help parents feel more comfortable when their children are away at residential schools.

Like anywhere else where children live, there are chances for abuse at a residential school (see Chapter 13 for information on abuse). Parents must encourage their children in residential schools to communicate their problems to teachers, house parents, and others.

Most deaf people who have studied in residential schools found the experience good. Even though they missed their families, the school gave them more opportunities to communicate with a larger group of people, and the deaf students created close communities with other students and the staff.

Day schools for the deaf

These day schools teach only deaf students. The children live at home with their families and continue to interact with hearing children and adults in their community.

Separate deaf classes in local schools

In some schools, deaf children spend the entire day in a separate classroom and see hearing children only during breaks. In other schools, deaf children spend part of the day in classrooms with hearing children, learning art or doing exercise. The ages and abilities of children in the special class may vary.

Benefits of learning only with other deaf children

* Most deaf schools and classrooms have teachers with special training to teach deaf children. These teachers can usually meet the deaf children's needs and attend to each child.

* Deaf children feel less isolated when they can communicate with all the people around them.

* Deaf children have opportunities to play, learn, develop social skills, and create friendships.

* Children can meet and interact with deaf adults who work at the school.

* Some deaf schools or classrooms also help deaf children get hearing tests and hearing aids.

Difficulties of learning only with other deaf children

* Deaf children who study in separate schools may not learn how to live and interact comfortably with people in the 'hearing world'.

* The schools may be far away and costly.

* Classes may include children of different ages. It may be difficult for teachers to meet their different needs.

Good schools meet deaf children's needs

All communities can have good schools for deaf and hearing children. It is not money, new buildings, or 'expert' teachers that make a good school. A good school pays attention to all the needs of its students and has committed teachers who help children of different hearing abilities learn and use language.

Schools that respond to the many different needs of deaf children can make a great difference in their lives.

Schools can cooperate with health care services and hospitals to provide hearing and eye tests, and hearing aids and eyeglasses. They can make the school available for vaccination campaigns to make it easy for parents to get the children vaccinated. And they can include nutrition and sanitation in the subjects they teach.

Schools can make time for deaf children to learn and play with hearing children, and not allow children to tease each other. When schools teach about the history and importance of deaf people and the deaf community they can help deaf children feel important and build self-esteem.

When schools first include children who are deaf, they often make mistakes, despite their good intentions. Schools have to learn about deafness, just like deaf children have to learn about schools. Here is a story of one family that persisted in getting their daughter an education and about the change that made in her life.

Oyuna's story

When Oyuna was 7 years old she started going to her neighborhood school, in a small town in Mongolia, with other children her age. Her parents had to work hard to convince the school to allow their deaf daughter to attend. The traditional belief in Mongolia is that deaf children are 'abnormal' and should not be with 'normal' children. Her parents felt very lucky that the director of the school agreed to admit her.

But even though Oyuna was going to school, she still had no means of communication except some gestures, pointing, and a few sounds. Her teacher at the neighborhood school could not communicate with her. It was soon obvious that Oyuna was not learning. Oyuna's parents began to lose hope because the only school for deaf children was in the capital city, very far from Oyuna's home.

How can Oyuna be expected to learn so far away from the support and love of her family? Especially when we have no way to explain the situation to her, or to be in contact with her.

Then a neighbor told them about a new program at another nearby school. A teacher at that school, whose own son was deaf, was helping to train the other teachers in basic sign language. The deaf children and the hearing children were all being taught in sign and in spoken words, in the same classroom.

Oyuna now goes to her new school happily every morning. The children in her class won a prize in a math competition among all schools in the town. And Oyuna got a prize for her good handwriting. Oyuna has changed from the sad, unsmiling girl who started school into a happy, playful child who often helps other children in her class.

GOOD SCHOOLS HAVE TEACHERS COMMITTED TO LEARNING

The most important qualities in a teacher are that she expects deaf children can do well in school and life, and that she takes the time to learn about each child's needs and abilities.

Experience makes the best teacher

A day school for the deaf in Tanzania had a teacher who was deaf herself. Even though she had no formal training as a

teacher, her patience and creativity helped to bring out the abilities of each child. Because the teacher could not hear their voices, she rested her hand on their shoulders to feel the vibration of the sound as they learned to speak. She also used sign language with them, helped them with their handwriting, and taught the children math by counting bottle caps.

The class was small, so the teacher was able to spend time with each child. She learned to identify and make use of their strongest abilities to help them learn.

Many people think that a teacher with special training is the best teacher for deaf children. This is not always true. Training about deafness does not automatically make a better teacher. Many teachers of the deaf do not have the opportunity to train in their own country, so they go away to learn in places that are very different from their own communities. The ideas they learn in another country may be difficult to use or may not work at all in the schools and communities back home.

A teacher who is trained to teach deaf children can be a resource for other teachers. Teachers of the deaf and teachers with experience teaching hearing children can learn from each other and build on what they know. This sharing of experience benefits all children.

DEAF ADULTS HELP DEAF CHILDREN LEARN

Deaf adults are probably the best teachers for deaf children. Good schools involve deaf adults in the classroom as teachers, translators, and assistants. Deaf adults understand the challenges deaf children face. Deaf adults can become role models for deaf children, and help create positive attitudes about deafness and deaf people.

Older children can help younger children learn to read and write.

CHILDREN CAN HELP EACH OTHER LEARN

Many children need help to learn difficult ideas. Deaf children often need extra help and attention to learn skills like reading and writing. Children — deaf and hearing, older and younger — can help each other learn skills and feel comfortable at school (pages 26, 137, and 138 include examples of how children can help each other).

Children can take part in their own education

A teacher in a school in Zambia encouraged the children to express themselves freely about what they wanted to learn. The teacher introduced ideas like voting in the classroom.

One week the children chose to learn about the reason why people fight and have wars. Another week they chose to learn about the weather and the reasons it rained during the wet season. As the weeks went by, many children became more interested in what they learned. They behaved better and attended school more regularly.

By the end of the school year, the children even went around the village to find other children who weren't attending school and encouraged them to come.

When children are involved in their education and work together to solve problems, they get an education better fitted to their needs. They feel confident about themselves, about what they learn, and about their ability to make a difference in the world!

FAMILY SUPPORT AT SCHOOL IS IMPORTANT

Parents and families have a major role in the education of their deaf child. Parents have experience they can share with the school to help teach deaf children. Parents can also work with the community to make schools better for deaf children. Schools with active parents' groups can talk about the educational and emotional needs of families with deaf children. Such schools are often better schools.

As parents become more aware of their child's right to education and ability to learn, they will themselves begin to make demands on local schools.

I am a little worried because I have never had a deaf child in my class, Mrs. Gomez.

Angela is a smart girl. I know she'll do well here. And I can teach you some signs until you find a deaf person to teach you and the class how to sign.

Good schools prepare a child to make a living

Many parents worry about the future for their children who are deaf or cannot hear well. How will they be able to earn a living and support themselves and their families?

Some schools for the deaf train their students in vocational skills they can use later to find a job or start a business. Both sewing and carpentry are common trades taught in vocational programs. There are also training courses that deaf children can go to after completing school, in computer skills, motor repair, printing technology, accounting, cooking, agriculture, and art. In fact, it is almost impossible to find a career in which a deaf person has not excelled!

At a residential school for the deaf in Romania, the children come from all over the country — sometimes from small villages more than 200 kilometers away. The children spend 9 months of the year at school, so it becomes a second home for them.

At school everyone uses hearing aids, learns speech and lip reading, and is taught to work with clay to make pottery. Many of the children leave the school when they are 14 years old and later earn their living as skilled potters.

Working together to help deaf children succeed

Deaf children can succeed when parents, schools, and communities work together to create a positive environment for them. Good education for these children depends on many things, including:

- whether children learn and use a language.
- whether there is good teaching, communication, and family participation.
- whether the community creates opportunities for deaf people to succeed.

The primary school where I teach has a popular carpentry class taught by a deaf man.

Parents, schools, and communities can work together to make sure vocational training is available to deaf youths, jobs are offered to deaf people, and loans or grants are available for small businesses.

Our group of deaf adults manage the railway station's restaurant. I think it is good for the hearing people we meet to learn to communicate with us. And if they don't learn, they don't eat!

Some communities even give lower taxes or financial assistance to businesses that employ workers who are deaf or do not hear well. Community organizations have established revolving loan plans that provide deaf craftspeople with funds to buy the basic equipment and materials to start their own small businesses. The loans are paid back little by little, so that the same money can be used to help another deaf person get started.

A young deaf person may be able to decide what skills she wants to learn, depending on her abilities and interests, as well as on the local resources, market, training opportunities, and other factors.

Several of my deaf friends who studied religion now serve as priests, and use sign language to communicate.

House painters find success

A network of deaf men in the south of India ran a house-painting business. People preferred to ask them to paint their houses as they did it faster than other painters. Babu, the leader, was skilled at negotiating and actively looked for new business. With many houses being built or remodeled, more and more people discovered the group of deaf men were skilled at their work, and they were in great demand.

While this book is about the importance of helping a deaf child as early as possible, it is also important to try to help deaf adults. Our communities are strongest when they look after all of us.

My name is Tsogu, and I live in Mongolia. Here is my story.

NEVER TOO LATE TO LEARN

Tsogu lost his hearing after a serious illness when he was 3 years old. As he grew older, he stayed at home while his sisters and brothers went off to school. Tsogu's family used a few home signs to communicate with

him, but he spent most of his time alone, taking care of the family's horses, sheep, and goats.

Tsogu was a good herdsman, but he was so isolated. We didn't want his world to be so limited.

We wanted him to be able to make friends, to read and write, and maybe learn a trade so he could have a better life.

One day his parents learned about a new class, started by a community group, for deaf adults who had never gone to school. After studying hard there for 2 years, Tsogu was finally able to communicate easily with his classmates, and to read, write, and do math.

Tsogu decided he wanted to learn a skilled trade like some of his friends from the same program. He was accepted at a vocational training school to learn how to be a carpenter.

With a good job, I was able to think about marrying and starting a family.

And our little girl has her father's curiosity and determination!

Chapter 13
Preventing child sexual abuse

It might seem strange to find information about sexual abuse in a book on helping children who cannot hear well. But, sadly, children who are deaf are even more at risk for sexual abuse than children who are not deaf. So it is very important for families with deaf children, and those who care for or teach deaf children, to know about it.

Keep our children safe

No one has the right to use a child for sex.

- *Not a family member (child or adult)*
- *Not a family friend*
- *Not a neighbor*
- *Not a stranger*
- *Not a teacher*
- *Not a caregiver*

Not anyone!

We parents need to talk about sexual abuse — with each other and with our children.

Talking about it is the first step in stopping it. Silence only protects abusers.

Yet it is hard to talk about sexual abuse. In many places:

- people do not know what sexual abuse is, how it happens, and the harm it causes.
- people are uncomfortable talking about sex.
- people do not want to believe that sexual abuse happens to very young children, so they do not think or talk about it.
- rules or customs limit who can talk to children about sex, what can be said, and when such conversations can happen.

**Every child should be safe from sexual abuse.
Keeping children safe from abuse is every adult's responsibility.**

Some facts about child sexual abuse

Child sexual abuse means using a child for some kind of sexual activity. Sexual abuse can happen to any child. It happens in all communities, and in rich and poor families. It happens to both girls and boys. Most sexual abuse happens to children older than 5 years, but it happens to younger children too.

We do not know exactly how common sexual abuse is, since many children do not tell what happens to them. But it is possible that as many as 1 out of every 4 children in the world is sexually abused.

There are many ways children can be abused. Some are:

Abuse when a child is touched

- oral sex (when a man puts his penis in a child's mouth)

- kissing or hugging a child in a sexual way

- sexual intercourse or anal sex (when a man puts his penis in a child's vagina or anus)

- touching a child's genitals (sexual parts) or making a child touch an adult's or an older child's genitals

- forcing a child to become a prostitute (take money for doing sex)

Abuse when a child is not touched

- using sexual talk or pictures to shock a child, make her sexually excited, or make her familiar with sex

- making a child hear or watch sex between other people

- making a child pose for sex pictures (pornography)

- making a child look at pornography

Most sexual abusers are men. And most abused children are abused by someone they know, like a relative, a family friend, or a neighbor. Abuse is rarely done by a stranger. Sometimes the abuse goes on for a long time, even for years.

Not all people who abuse children sexually use physical force. Sometimes a person uses a position of trust or influence to make a child have sex. He might use persuasion and 'kindness', threats and bullying, or give gifts or treats. (An abuser may even be a deaf person who befriends the child.) Whether someone uses physical force, threats, or 'kindness' to make a child have sex, **the result of the abuse is still very damaging to the child.**

Why are deaf children at risk for sexual abuse?

All children are at some risk for sexual abuse because they must trust adults and older children, and depend on them for care. Children are taught that 'good children' do as they are told. This makes it difficult to say no to adults. Very young children also have no way to know how adults normally behave, or what is acceptable adult behavior.

Deaf children are especially at risk for sexual abuse because:

- Society, in general, values people with disabilities less than others. So an abuser may think it is okay to use a deaf child for sex. And because girls are usually valued less than boys, deaf girls are valued even less than deaf boys. So deaf girls are most at risk.

- Deaf people use touch to communicate — for example, to get someone's attention. A deaf child may think someone's touch is okay even if it is not.

- Deaf children have less information than hearing children, but are just as curious. They may also be isolated or feel lonely, which makes them easy targets for abusers.

I want Radha to be safe. But how can I teach her to protect herself? My mother never talked to me about this.

I know what you mean. My daughter Mishiri also can't hear well. And I'm never sure if she understands me. Can we think of ways to explain this to them?

- Deaf children who have limited communication may have learned to do what others want without asking why.

- Deaf children who have limited communication skills may not fully understand what you tell them about their safety.

- Limited communication also makes it harder for deaf children to tell anyone about abuse. Someone may abuse a deaf child because he knows she will not be able to speak about the experience. Deaf children may only be able to communicate with family members or others who look after them. If the abuser is also a family member, caregiver, or teacher, the child may not feel safe telling anyone.

Sexual abuse causes lasting harm

Sexual abuse harms a child at the moment when the abuse happens and can continue to harm a victim throughout his or her life. This is especially true if a child is unable to talk about the abuse or receive help, support, and treatment.

Lasting physical harm

Lasting physical harm can be caused by sexually transmitted infections (STIs). An abuser can infect a child with HIV/AIDS and hepatitis, which cannot be cured. Other STIs, if left untreated, can cause future problems with pregnancy, cancer, and death from severe infection. Children who get STIs from sexual abuse often do not show any signs and so they do not get treatment.

Damage to a child's development

Children who have been abused sexually are likely to feel a great deal of guilt, shame, and anger. Many victims of sexual abuse are unable to trust other people. Victims are also likely to have poor self-esteem — they feel they are not valuable and not worthy of being treated with respect.

Cycles of abuse

Children who have been abused sexually may continue to be abused by others throughout their lives. Because of their experience of abuse as children, they may grow up to believe that sex is the only way to get affection or security. Being treated badly and being abused sexually can become a pattern in their lives.

Also, without support and help to heal from the abuse, boys who have been abused may become abusers themselves when they grow older. This cycle of abuse creates another generation of victims and future offenders.

An abused child may grow up to abuse others

GROWS UP   *GROWS UP*

Without help, the cycle of abuse continues...

The harm caused by child sexual abuse is not just to children and their families, but to entire communities. For example, people who are unfairly shamed and isolated because of sexual abuse can sometimes become destructive or violent, or turn to alcohol or drug abuse.

Preventing sexual abuse

How we are treated by others affects our self-esteem. When children are treated as helpless, and hopeless, they see themselves as helpless, and hopeless. So we must teach children to feel good about themselves so they will be confident and better able to protect themselves.

Leave me alone!

> To keep children safe, we must give them the knowledge, skills, and confidence to reject sexual misbehavior — even from bigger, stronger, and more powerful people.

HELP YOUR CHILD UNDERSTAND AND COMMUNICATE ABOUT SEXUAL ABUSE

Deaf children learn most easily when they see things. Signs, body movements, and expressions on the face, along with picture cards, puppet shows, and role plays, can all help you teach a deaf child how to be safe from sexual abuse. Help her understand that:

- some kinds of touches are not okay (a handshake is okay, a hug may be okay, but touching genitals is not okay, and putting a penis in a child's mouth is not okay).

- she should tell you if something she does not like happens to her.

- she can refuse if someone tries to touch her sexually.

Ideas like 'private', 'secret', 'trust', 'safe', and signs for them, are hard to explain to young children, especially if they are deaf. Remember that you will have to explain these ideas over and over.

Use different signs, gestures, pictures, and words until you feel sure your child understands. Act out situations with your child, or use dolls or pictures to try as many ways of showing these ideas as you can.

*This man is touching the little girl in a **bad way**. If this ever happens to you, you come **tell mama**!*

Tell mama.

Some examples of signs that may help you explain sexual abuse

These signs are in *American Sign Language*. Remember, the signs in your own country's sign language may be different.

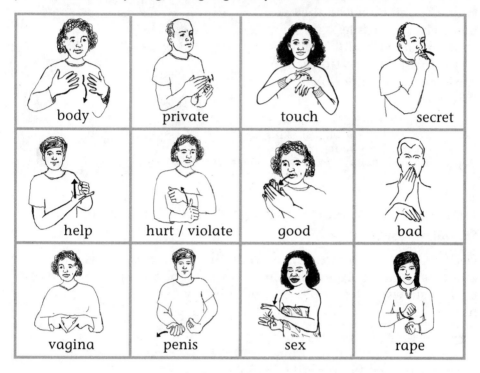

body	private	touch	secret
help	hurt / violate	good	bad
vagina	penis	sex	rape

HELP CHILDREN NAME AND DESCRIBE ABUSERS

Give your children sign names for people in their lives. Practice noticing details about people and places and communicate about them with your child. Teach your child describing words, like tall, short, hairy, fat, thin, and others. When a child can describe a person, she can describe an abuser.

Give everyone a sign name

One of our little girls, a 6-year-old deaf girl, was raped. The police asked us to question her about who had done this to her. She was not able to give an answer. One reason is that she does not have sign names for everyone around her. We are now encouraging parents to give everyone who comes into their lives a sign name. In this way, anyone who hurt the child could be named and brought to justice.

— Nzeve Deaf Children's Center, Zimbabwe, Africa

ACTIVITIES

Here are more activities to help your child be safer from sexual abuse.

▶ Ways to help your child understand that some parts of the body should be private

Explain to your child that her body belongs to her alone, and that some parts of her body are more private than others. Explain that adults and older children should not touch her genitals or private

*Your bottom is a **private** part of the body.*

parts, and that she should not touch an adult's private parts, even if asked to. Use dolls, puppets, or pictures, and show approval or disapproval by your body movement and facial expression.

Also, explain that if someone asks your child to watch private things or look at pictures of private things, that is not okay either.

When your child is between 3 and 5 years old, teach about genitals and other private parts of the body, and about the differences between boys' and girls' bodies.

These are difficult ideas to teach, so use different methods to try to make sure your child understands. Teaching can happen naturally, for example while your child is getting dressed. You can also use or make a doll to teach about body parts.

▶ How to help your child learn to make noise or yell for help

Many deaf children do not like to use their voices. This is because they are laughed at or told they sound funny when they do. Explain to your child that it is okay to shout if someone is bothering him and he needs help.

If someone hurts you, yell or say 'no'. Let's practice yelling out loud.

Teach your child that he should shout 'No, no!', or 'Help!', or stamp his feet if an adult or older child tries to hurt him. He can also scream, bite, and struggle. Use dolls or play-acting to show him what you mean.

▶ *How to help your child learn to say no*

Deaf children often do not understand **why** they should do or not do certain things, or why things happen to them. They want to please people, and so they learn to obey without question. This can be a problem if someone tells them to do something that is wrong.

Help your child practice saying 'no'. First, try making up situations in which a child may want to say 'no'.

Later, talk about saying 'no' and where your child can get help.

Ask your child to tell you or another adult right away if someone asks him to do anything he feels uncomfortable doing.

▶ How to help your child understand that he or she does not always have to obey bigger people

Once a child has learned to say 'no', you can make up situations in which the child does not have to obey adults.

> Suppose an adult tells you to go outside and run after cars and buses in the road. Must you do it?

> No.

> Why not?

▶ How to help your child know where to go for help

Who can your child turn to? All children should have at least 3 people whom they can go to with problems. This could be their mother or father, older sister or brother, aunt, neighbor, or any other person both you and the child trust outside the family, like another child's mother.

Children should know that if one person is not available or will not pay attention, they should go to the next person. Tell those people that you are teaching the child to go to them for help if necessary. Practice with the child how to go to people for different kinds of help.

> Where could you go for help if I am at work? How about your Aunt Rose? Or Lisa's mother? Who else?

> To Nana.

How can I know if my child has been abused?

When young children are abused, they may be afraid to tell you. Often the abuser warns the child not to say anything. Sometimes the child fears he did something wrong. Or he may not know how to communicate what happened.

Since children do not always communicate about abuse, you need to watch for possible signs. The following signs are **not always** the result of abuse, but they should always cause concern, especially if a child shows several of the signs.

Some physical signs include:

- unexplained pain, swelling, redness or bleeding of the mouth, the genitals or around the anus area.

- torn or bloody underwear.

- difficulty passing urine or stool, or blood in the urine or stool.

- unusual discharge from the vagina, penis or anus, or a sexually transmitted infection (STI).

- bruises, headaches, or belly aches.

Sexually abused children may:

- stop bathing, or wash themselves more than usual, or refuse to get undressed.

- play sexually with other children or with toys, in a more knowing way or more often than you would expect for their age.

- know more about sex than other children their age.

Child victims of violence, including sexual abuse, may:

- seem very fearful, sensitive and watchful, or suddenly become afraid of certain people or places, or want to be only with their parents.

- be secretive or want to be alone most of the time.

- start acting in a younger, more baby-like way.

- become more violent and aggressive.

- try to run away from home.

- feel sad most of the time, or show no feelings at all.

- have difficulty sleeping because of bad dreams, fears of the dark, and bed-wetting.

- be afraid of touch or physical activities.

If you suspect abuse

Try to stay calm. Encourage your child to show you what has happened or what she knows.

To get more information, set up play situations with your child. Pay careful attention to what he shows you because he may not have enough words or signs to explain himself clearly. With your voice and your expressions, make sure your child knows you believe him and will not punish him.

If your child has been sexually abused

If your child has been sexually abused, you can help if you:

- believe what she shows or communicates with you. It may be difficult to believe that someone you know and trust has done this to your child, but children rarely make up stories about sexual abuse. Some abusers are very friendly to parents. That way they gain better access to the children and it keeps the parents from reporting the abuse.

- praise her for telling you. Children need to know that they have done the right thing by communicating about the abuse.

- reassure her that the abuse is not her fault and that you are not angry with her. Use as many different ways of communicating this as possible.

- protect your child's safety. Try to prevent future contact between the child and the abuser. If this is not possible, make sure you or someone who knows what happened is always with your child when the abuser is present.

- treat physical health problems from the abuse. Try to get your child tested for sexually transmitted infections, even if she does not have any signs. Some sexually transmitted infections do not have any signs, or the signs do not show until a child is older.

As a parent, you also need help. Parents feel many emotions including disbelief, anger, and sadness when they learn their child has been abused. Parents may blame themselves or each other for what happened to their child. It can help to talk about these feelings with someone you trust. Be patient with yourself. It may take a long time for these feelings to change.

There is no shame to the family if a child has been abused. Abuse is a crime — like theft — and was not caused by the family.

To make all children in the community safer

Most people are not comfortable talking about sexual abuse, accepting that children are not safe, or discussing the harmful effects of sexual abuse. Yet sexual abuse can only be prevented if everyone can talk about it.

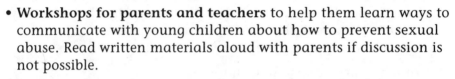

Programs in schools and community meetings can educate the entire community about sexual abuse. Acting out short plays or skits about the effects of sexual abuse sometimes makes it easier for people to discuss abuse as a group.

Here are some community-wide ways to work on preventing sexual abuse:

- **Workshops for parents and teachers** to help them learn ways to communicate with young children about how to prevent sexual abuse. Read written materials aloud with parents if discussion is not possible.

- **Training for teachers, staff working in schools, doctors and health workers** so they can notice signs a child may have been abused, and learn how to talk with a child who may be a victim of abuse. Hold workshops with school staff to discuss the ethics of working with children.

- **Education for school children** to prevent sexual abuse. This education can also include age-appropriate education on healthy sexuality.

- **Reporting abuse when it happens** can help prevent it in the future. Find out what procedures exist for reporting child sexual abuse and make sure this information is available to parents, teachers, health workers, and others who may learn about the sexual abuse of a child. Work to create a procedure if none exists.

The more people know about the problem of sexual abuse, the more we can prevent it from happening to our children.

Chapter 14
Support for parents and caregivers

All over the world, parents and other family members work very hard caring for their young children. And when a family has a child who cannot hear, there is the extra responsibility of making sure he gets everything he needs to grow well. The extra work will make a big difference to the child, but it can be very stressful and tiring for the parents. This chapter has information to help families and caregivers of deaf children find ways to cope with their situation and care for themselves as well as for their children.

Because we share our lives with our children, everything that happens to them affects us deeply. Many families with deaf children feel helpless or fear the future. If parents join together to support each other, they can improve the lives of their deaf children. They can also work as a group to get their community to better support all children who have hearing problems.

When you first learn your child cannot hear well

Learning that a child cannot hear well or is deaf can be very upsetting, even for families who have relatives who are deaf or cannot hear well. This is natural. You may have feelings of:

- worry about what to do

I don't know anything about deafness. How could I possibly help my child?

- fears of what it means to be deaf and fears about the future

How will my child get married or earn a living?

- denial

My child will hear well if I just find the right treatment.

- anger at what has happened

It's not fair that this happened to my family.

- loneliness

No one else knows what this is like. No one can help.

- guilt about what you might have done to cause the deafness

If I had eaten better during my pregnancy, this would never have happened.

- shame because your child is deaf

What will our neighbors think?

- sadness, helplessness, or no feelings at all (depression)

I feel so hopeless...

- accepting it as fate or punishment

We can't do anything to change a curse. It is just our fate.

Understanding your emotions

Parents, other family members, and caregivers will react to the emotions they feel in different ways. It is best to let each person feel the emotions in his or her own way, without judgment.

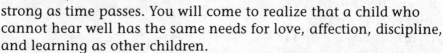

Touli feels angry that the baby is deaf, but I feel sad all the time.

Emotions such as worry, loneliness, or fear will become less strong as time passes. You will come to realize that a child who cannot hear well has the same needs for love, affection, discipline, and learning as other children.

What if she can't learn like the other children?

These emotions will return to you at important times in your child's life, like when she starts school. This does not mean something is wrong. It just means you are going through another period of adapting to her deafness.

These strong emotions can help you take action to make your child's life better. For example, loneliness may encourage you to reach out to deaf adults in your community or to other families with deaf children. Anger may give you energy to help organize other parents to persuade the government to provide education for deaf children.

When you accept that your child cannot hear well, you can begin to love your child as she is. And, like all children, she will give you much support, pleasure, and joy!

Look at how much fun they are having! How did I ever think Delphine would be a burden to our family?

Managing the stress of caregiving

Being a parent of any child is hard work.
And if your child cannot hear well or is deaf, then there is even more work. For example, families must teach deaf children things that other children learn on their own, from hearing people talk.

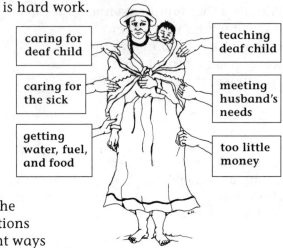

caring for deaf child

caring for the sick

getting water, fuel, and food

teaching deaf child

meeting husband's needs

too little money

It can be difficult to find time and energy for this extra work. This page and the next one have some suggestions from families about different ways that have helped them manage this stress.

CARING FOR CAREGIVERS

Parents and other caregivers will be able to look after children better if they also have some time to relax. Simple things — like going to the market, visiting friends or relatives, talking with friends, having a massage, or being part of a community group — can all be helpful. Remember, you can help your children more when you feel well.

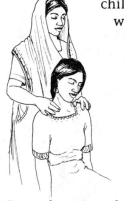

Remember to care for each other. Being a parent is hard work.

Sometimes it is helpful for a group of parents to get together to talk with each other about any difficulties they may be having. If some have difficulty saying things to others in a group, perhaps they can make up songs, poems, or stories about their situation. Drawing and painting pictures can also help some people express their thoughts and feelings without using words. They do not have to be 'real' artists to do this.

Many communities have beliefs and traditions that help calm the body and mind, as well as build inner strength. Practicing these traditions may help you take better care of yourself.

prayer

meditation

exercise or
martial arts

Parents' groups

A parents' group changes Irlandita's life

A mother in Nicaragua, named Rosa, began to suspect something was not right with her daughter Irlandita. Irlandita did not respond when her name was called, and only reacted to very loud noises.

Worried for her daughter, Rosa took Irlandita to a doctor when she was 16 months old. The doctor was very cold to her, and said only, "Your child can't hear anything. Bring her back when she's 5 years old and we will see if anything can be done for her." Rosa left feeling more frightened and lost than she had been before the visit.

On the way home she met a friend who suggested that she make an appointment with Los Pipitos, a community organization. Los Pipitos was started by a group of parents who wanted their children with disabilities to have the opportunity to develop fully.

Although the doctor and staff at Los Pipitos gave Rosa the same diagnosis — that her daughter was deaf — they also gave her hope for the future. They explained how with special help and extra support from her family, Irlandita could develop just like a child who hears normally. With the support of other parents at Los Pipitos, Rosa began to feel confident that she could make a difference in Irlandita's life.

Now Rosa is an active member of Los Pipitos and she works to give other parents the same help and friendship that she herself found when she needed it.

Thanks to the support of her family, and the care given at Los Pipitos, Irlandita is an expressive, caring, happy, intelligent, and confident girl. She can communicate and is able to attend a regular school.

With the help of Los Pipitos and a lot of effort at home, we have come a long way in 3 years. To other parents I would say, 'I could do it, and you can too! Try!'

STARTING A GROUP

If you know there are other parents with deaf children in your community, but there is no parents' group in your area, it may be up to you to start one. Some of the strongest, most active parents' groups began because of one person's idea. As a group, parents can work together to solve problems. Parents working together can do more than if they each work alone.

> Our group sent someone to talk with the National Association of the Deaf in the city. Now a field worker who is deaf regularly visits our village.

- Find 2 or more parents or caregivers who want to start a group. If you do not know other families with deaf children, you may be able to find parents of children with other disabilities. Or a health worker may know of parents in nearby communities.

- Plan when and where to meet. It helps to choose a place where everyone will be comfortable talking, perhaps a room in a school, health center, cooperative, or place of worship. At the first meeting, discuss why you are meeting and what you hope to do.

- Probably one person will be the leader of the first few meetings. But it is important that no one person makes decisions for the group. Everyone should have a chance to talk. Try to keep the discussion focused on the main reasons for the meeting. After the first few meetings, take turns leading the group. Having different people lead each meeting will help shy members participate.

LEARNING TO SUPPORT EACH OTHER

Even when people know each other well, it may take time to feel comfortable talking about feelings, experiences, and the challenges of raising a child who is deaf or cannot hear well. These things take practice.

> Why should we share our troubles with the whole neighborhood?

> Omar, who can help us better than our friends? At least we all can face these problems together.

Here are some suggestions to help group members feel comfortable and to trust in each other:

Listen carefully to what others say, without judging them. Think about how you want others to listen to you, and then try to listen to them in the same way.

Can you try to explain it again?

Pearl, I'm not sure I understand what you are saying.

Try not to tell other people what to do. You can help others understand how they are feeling, and share your own experiences. But everyone must make their own decisions about the best way to care for their children.

Vladir gets very angry if we try to change our daily routine. Do you have any ideas that will help us?

Paulo would get so angry at little things when he was that age. It is easier now.

How did you help Paulo learn to control his temper? That is something we are facing with our daughter.

Respect each person's privacy. Never tell others what the group talks about unless each person says that is okay.

Planning for action

Parents working together can take action to solve many problems. Here are some useful steps for taking action:

1. Choose a problem that most people in the group feel is important. Although many changes are probably needed, your group may be more effective if it works on one problem at a time. At first, pick a problem that your group has a good chance of solving quickly. Then, as the group learns how to work together, you can work on more complicated problems.

2. Decide how you want to solve the problem. List many ways the problem could be solved and then pick the one that best uses your group's strengths and resources.

We could hire someone to take care of our children. Maybe we can find a person who knows sign language.

We could take turns. Each family could care for all the children one day a week.

Arti is looking for work.

3. Make a plan. Members of the group will need to do different things to get the job done. Try to set a date when each task should be finished.

Guddi, you are part of the deaf community. Can you see if there is someone who is looking for work who knows sign language?

I'll find out how much we would need to pay someone.

I'll ask Arti if she would want to learn some signs from me.

4. When you meet together, talk about how the work is going. Adjust your plan as needed if difficulties arise.

Have we found anyone who knows sign language?

No, not yet. Not many people know sign language.

But Arti is eager to learn sign and to care for our children.

A GROUP WITH FEW RESOURCES CAN STILL MAKE A DIFFERENCE!

We believe the whole community — neighborhood, village, city, or nation — is responsible for supporting families with children who have disabilities. But sometimes it takes parents working together to make the larger community take that responsibility. As the following story about a group of determined parents in South Africa shows, when people cooperate and put their resources together, they can overcome obstacles and make something where there was nothing!

Building resources — the power of determination

In a city in South Africa, children with learning disabilities rarely played with other children or attended school. Many parents could not work outside the home because the local day care centers did not want to include their children. The centers told the parents who approached them, "You cannot tell us what to do!" and "We have no facilities for teaching these children."

A group of parents — all unemployed mothers, many with little or no formal education — got together and decided they must do something for these children and their families. They decided that 1 or 2 of them would look after all the children so that the others would be free to look for work.

We had no funding, no special resources. We agreed that parents would send something with their children — half a cabbage, a carrot, or a potato — whatever we could manage.

With these ingredients, those of us who were caring for the children would cook soup.

The mothers organized a schedule for caring for the children. One of them volunteered to cook. One became a teacher. Others looked for work that they could do at home. Parents who managed to find work began to contribute a little to those who cared for the children and to the growing day care center. One parent who worked began to buy books for the children.

A social worker heard about the group and came to see what they were doing. She was able to get the local government to give some money to pay the mothers who took care of the children.

With the only resource the mothers had — determination — they were able to establish a day care center for their children, and they were also able to earn a living!

Working together for change

Parents' groups work on many kinds of projects. They may try to improve the economic conditions of families, the attitudes of communities, or the government's laws and services for deaf children — all as a way to help their children. To get more resources for their children, a parents group can:

- find ways to get funding for new projects to help deaf children.

- help parents develop new job skills.

- offer workshops on ways to teach and help their children.

- share information about hearing aids.

- organize sign language classes.

- bring hearing and deaf people together.

These mothers learned how to sew clothing so they could earn more money, work closer to home, and spend more time with their children.

Many parents' groups work to educate the rest of the community about deafness. They often work together with people who are deaf. The groups use workshops, radio programs, newsletters, billboards, street theater, and posters to help others understand more about deafness.

Some parents' groups work to improve government programs and laws for children who are deaf. They contact people in the government, like the ministers of health and education. They tell them about services their community needs, or about laws needed to protect children who are deaf or have hearing problems. They write letters, pass around petitions, or organize protests if government officials do not improve conditions for their children.

MORE SCHOOLS FOR OUR CHILDREN

MORE LAWS TO PROTECT OUR CHILDREN

MORE SERVICES FOR DEAF CHILDREN

Chapter 15
Why children lose their hearing and what we can do

There are millions of children all over the world who are deaf or have hearing problems. Most of them are poor. Out of every 3 children with hearing problems, 2 live in poor countries. Their deafness is often caused by infection and poor nutrition. For most of these children, deafness could have been prevented by taking care of basic needs — like good food, clean drinking water, a safe, clean place to live, and access to health care.

He had many untreated ear infections.

She did not have enough iodine in her food and water.

Her mother did not have enough food when she was pregnant.

He had measles.

This chapter can help you learn about the causes and medical treatments for some hearing problems. To prevent deafness, communities must work together to solve the social causes that medicine cannot fix.

Children's health and hearing benefit when communities have clean air (free of smoke and dust) and good sanitation, and are free of violence. Good health care, including health education, immunizations, and early treatment of illness, is key to protecting children's hearing.

Wrong beliefs
Some people believe a child is deaf because the parents did something wrong. Other people believe a child is deaf because someone has done evil to the child's mother, and the child is 'witched'. Neither of these things causes deafness.

How the ear works

The ear is made up of 3 main parts: the outer ear, the middle ear, and the inner ear. The outer ear is the part you can see. The middle and inner ear are inside the head and cannot be seen. All 3 parts of the ear are needed for a child to hear.

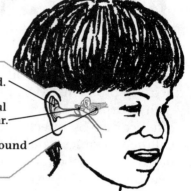

The outer ear picks up a sound.

It travels through the ear canal and ear drum to the middle ear.

Then the inner ear sends the sound to the brain so he can hear it.

The brain then helps a child understand what the sound means.

Problems in any part of the ear can cause deafness

Problems in the outer ear and middle ear:
- ear infections (page 193)
- something blocks sound from traveling through the ear (page 198)
- injury (page 214)

Problems in the inner ear and the nerve leading to the brain:
- infection during pregnancy (page 208)
- baby's brain damaged during labor or birth (page 212)
- childhood illness such as meningitis (page 201)
- lack of iodine in mother's food during pregnancy (page 207)
- medicines that damage hearing (page 206)
- deafness passed down in families (page 214)
- damage from loud noises (page 213)

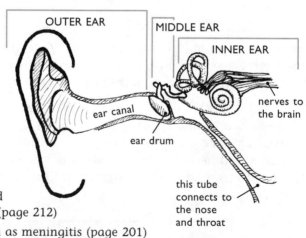

OUTER EAR

MIDDLE EAR

INNER EAR

ear canal

ear drum

nerves to the brain

this tube connects to the nose and throat

Ear infection

Ear infections are one of the most common childhood illnesses and without treatment, they can cause permanent hearing loss. Ear infections often start with an infection of the nose and throat. The infection travels from the throat along the tube into the middle ear.

Children get these infections easily because the tube from the throat to the ear is shorter than in adults. When the ear is infected, the fluid and infection cannot drain out of the middle ear. And if a child has a cold, the tube from the throat that leads to the middle ear often gets blocked. As children grow older and stronger, they develop more resistance and get fewer colds and throat infections.

SUDDEN EAR INFECTIONS (ACUTE)

Sudden middle-ear infection can occur at any age, and is common even in babies and infants. The child may cry, be irritable, and have a fever. Often the infection gets better in 1 or 2 days without any treatment. A painkiller will help the child feel better but will not cure the infection. Sometimes an antibiotic is needed to cure the infection (see page 195). The ear drum may burst and pus leaks out through a small hole. This hole usually heals quickly.

LONG-LASTING EAR INFECTIONS (CHRONIC)

When children do not get treatment for repeated sudden ear infections, the infection can become long-lasting. An ear infection is long-lasting if pus drains from the ear and there is discharge for 14 days or more. This can damage the ear drum. The ear drum may become pulled inward or have a hole that does not heal. Both of these problems lead to more infection with discharge.

Without proper and early medical care, children may lose their hearing, suffer from dizziness, weakness on one side of the face, or an abscess draining behind or below the ear. Rarely, an ear infection may also cause a serious complication like a brain abscess or meningitis (see page 204).

More poor children lose their hearing because of ear infections than any other cause. Hearing loss due to ear infections can be prevented by improving general health and living conditions, and by access to medical care. Every community needs people trained to identify ear infections early, or clinics or hospitals that are affordable and easy to get to.

Glue ear

Sometimes after sudden ear infections, thick and sticky fluid collects in the middle ear (this is called glue ear). Glue ear does not usually hurt and drains away down the tube to the nose after a few weeks, but sometimes it lasts for years. Glue ear often affects both ears and it makes the child partially deaf as long as it lasts. Most cases of glue ear will heal without treatment. But if there is any pain, give an antibiotic by mouth as for acute infection (see pages 195 to 196).

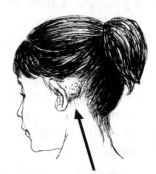

Signs of ear infection:

- Pain — a young child may cry, rub the side of his head, or pull on his ear

- Fever between 37.7° and 40°C (100° and 104°F)

- Runny nose, sore throat, cough

fluid

- Fluid may drain from the ear. It may be yellow, white, watery or sticky. The fluid may have some blood in it. A heavy flow of sticky, clear fluid is probably from a hole in the ear drum. This fluid may stop with medicines, but it can happen every time the child has a cold, or puts his ears under water or swims.

A slight fluid discharge that smells and may be yellow or green is probably from damage to the ear drum. An operation may be needed to repair the ear drum.

- Hearing loss — temporary or permanent — in one or both ears

- Sometimes nausea and vomiting

- Sometimes infection spreads to the bone behind the ear (mastoiditis). This is very painful and antibiotics must be given. **Go to a hospital!**

mastoiditis

Different signs may be present at different times — for example, the pain may stop when fluid starts flowing out of the ear.

Check the ear in 3 to 4 months after any ear infection, even if there is no pain and check the child's hearing (see pages 50 to 58).

TREATING EAR INFECTIONS

To treat sudden (acute) ear infections

For pain and fever:

- give paracetamol (acetaminophen) by mouth
3 to 4 times a day as needed.

  age 3 months to 1 year.................. 60 to 120 mg

  age 1 to 5 years .... 120 to 250 mg

  age 6 to 12 years .... 250 to 500 mg

- give ibuprofen by mouth.

  age 1 to 2 years .... 50 mg, 3 to 4 times a day

  age 3 to 7 years .... 100 mg, 3 to 4 times a day

  age 8 to 12 years .... 200 mg, 3 to 4 times a day

  Note: Do not give ibuprofen to children younger than 1 year old
  or who weigh less than 7 kg.

For the infection:

- give amoxicillin by mouth, for 3 to 10 days.

  age 2 years or less .... 125 mg, 3 times a day

  age 3 years or more .... 250 mg, 3 times a day

- give amoxicillin with clavulanic acid as syrup (preferably sugar-free)
by mouth, for 5 days.

  age less than 6 years .... amoxicillin 125 mg with
  clavulanic acid 31 mg, 3 times a day.

  (If syrup is not available give half a tablet of amoxicillin
  250 mg with clavulanic acid 125 mg, 3 times a day.)

  age 6 to 12 years .... amoxicillin 250 mg with
  clavulanic acid 62 mg, 3 times a day.

  (If syrup is not available give 1 tablet of amoxicillin
  250 mg with clavulanic acid 125 mg, 3 times a day.)

When will he feel better?

The ibuprofen will help his pain right away while the antibiotic treats his infection over the next week.

Make sure you give all the antibiotic or the infection may come back.

Other treatments for sudden (acute) ear infections

If the child is allergic to penicillin or the treatment is not working:

- give co-trimoxazole (trimethoprim + sulfamethoxazole) by mouth, for 3 to 10 days.

  age 6 weeks to 5 months .... 120 mg, 2 times a day

  age 6 months to 5 years .... 240 mg, 2 times a day

  age 6 to 12 years .... 480 mg, 2 times a day

   or

- give cefuroxime by mouth, for 5 days.

  age 2 years or less .... 125 mg, 2 times a day

  age more than 2 years................... 250 mg, 2 times a day

  or

- give cefaclor by mouth, for 3 to 10 days.

  age 1 month to 1 year .... 62.5 mg, 3 times a day

  age 1 to 5 years .... 125 mg, 3 times a day

  age more than 5 years................... 250 mg, 3 times a day

   or

- give erythromycin by mouth, for 3 to 10 days.

  age 1 year or less........................... 125 mg, 4 times a day

  age 2 to 8 years .... 250 mg, 4 times a day

  age more than 8 years................... 250 to 500 mg, 4 times a day

If there is fluid draining from the ear, wipe it away, but **do not stick anything in the ear to clean it**. Encourage the child to rest and drink a lot of liquids. The child can bathe, but should not put his ears under water or swim for at least 2 weeks after he is well.

If you think the child may have a complication, take him to a hospital. If you suspect meningitis, give medicine immediately (see page 204).

To treat long-lasting or repeated (chronic) ear infections
(discharge for 2 weeks or more)

- Give antibiotic ear drops for 1 week (2 to 3 drops, 3 times a day) such as ciprofloxacin, framycetin, gentamicin, gramicidin, neomycin, polymyxin B, or ofloxacin.

Sometimes it helps to give an antibiotic by mouth at the same time as the ear drop. Use the same antibiotic as for sudden ear infection (see page 195).

Antibiotic drops should not be used for longer than 10 days, or repeated frequently, as they can cause hearing loss themselves. But chronic ear infections are more likely to cause hearing loss than antibiotic drops.

If the discharge continues or returns, or if antibiotic ear drops are not available:

• give antiseptic ear drops such as vinegar (see page 201) or povidone iodine (betadine).

for all ages ....2 drops in the ear, 2 times a day for 2 weeks

then give...2 drops in the ear, 1 time a day (before going to sleep), for several weeks or months

---

Repeat the same treatment if infection and discharge occurs again. A health worker or doctor can teach parents to clean out the discharge with cotton wool before each dose of ear drops.

Keep all water out of the ear. Carefully dry the ear two times daily with cotton wool or gauze for several weeks (until it remains dry).

Sometimes an operation is needed to repair the ear drum. This is done by a specially-trained health worker in a hospital, usually when the child is at least 10 years old.

PREVENTING EAR INFECTIONS

To prevent ear infections, breastfeed babies — for up to 2 years if possible. Breast milk helps a baby fight infection. Breastfeeding also helps strengthen the muscles that keep the tubes between the throat and middle ear open.

HIV/AIDS and breastfeeding

If a woman has HIV/AIDS, sometimes this disease can pass to a baby through her breast milk. But if she does not have access to clean water, her baby is more likely to die from diarrhea, dehydration, and malnutrition than from AIDS. Only a mother can evaluate the conditions in her home and community and decide what to do.

Babies older than 6 months have less danger of dying from diarrhea because they are bigger and stronger. A woman with HIV/AIDS who has breastfed her baby should stop at 6 months and feed him with other milks and foods. This way the baby will have less risk of getting HIV/AIDS.

Other ways to prevent ear infections

- If a baby has to be fed from a bottle or a cup, be sure to keep his head higher than his stomach as you feed him. If he lies down while feeding, the milk can flow from his throat into the tubes and into his middle ears, helping to cause infection.

- Teach a child to wipe his nose instead of blowing it. If he does blow his nose, he should do it gently.

- As much as possible, keep children away from smoke, including smoke from stoves and cooking fires. Smoke can make the tube between the throat and middle ear swell and close. Then fluid builds up in the middle ear and it can get infected.

- When your child has a cold, find out if he also has ear pain. As much as possible, keep your child away from people with colds.

Something blocks sound from traveling through the ear

Children can lose their hearing temporarily when something like hard ear wax or another object blocks sound from traveling through the ear.

EAR WAX PLUGS

Ear wax helps to prevent infection. It forms a protective layer on the delicate skin in the ear, helps keep the ear clean, and makes the skin waterproof. Usually, the wax gradually moves out of the ear, carrying with it trapped dirt and dust, but sometimes the wax builds up, hardens, and becomes stuck. This can happen because of cleaning ears with cotton buds (small sticks with cotton on the ends) or other objects that push the wax deep into the ear canals. This hard plug of ear wax keeps sounds from traveling easily through the ear and can cause an infection. Ear wax can also be a problem for children who use hearing aids, so these children's ears should be checked regularly and their hearing aids should be cleaned if necessary.

Signs:

- A child seems to hear less well than usual.

- Sometimes you can see the plug of hard wax in the ear.

- Sometimes the wax plug or infection around it may cause the child to have an earache with pus draining out.

A small amount of wax is normal and should not be touched.

For ear wax

If there is no pain, fever, or discharge from the ear, too much wax or a wax plug can be removed by washing out the ear with warm water.

1. First, soften the wax by putting several drops of warm, mild vegetable oil into the ear. Keep the child lying down on her side with her ear up for 15 minutes.

2. Next, wash the ear well by pouring several cups of clean, warm (not hot) water into the ear with a spout. If this does not work, use a syringe with no needle (preferably 20 ml size) or a rubber bulb syringe to squirt the warm water into the ear.
   WARNING: Do not squirt water in the ear if there is fluid draining from the ear!

   - Remove the needle from the syringe and fill the syringe with warm water from a cup.

   - Gently pull the ear away from the head. Carefully squirt the water into the ear canal. **Do not point the syringe directly down the ear toward the ear drum. Point it sideways toward the back wall of the ear canal. Stop if your child starts to feel dizzy.**

   With a bulb syringe, do not put the tip far or tightly into the ear canal. Try to keep the tip steady in the ear while squeezing the bulb.

Repeat this 3 times a week for 2 weeks and then once again after 1 or 2 weeks. Doing it more often can damage the ear.

Get medical advice for a hard plug of wax that does not dissolve easily.

INSECT IN THE EAR

Signs:

- The child may say he can feel or hear scratching, crawling, or bumping in the ear.

- Fluid or pus may drain from the ear.

- A child may hear less well than usual in the affected ear.

For an insect in the ear

Fill the ear with clean mineral or vegetable oil. The insect may drown and then float out. If this does not work, try to wash the ear in the same way as for removing wax.

For objects in the ear

Children sometimes put small objects into their ears. If the object is soft, and if a health worker or you can easily reach behind the object with a small wire hook, try carefully removing it.

Do not use tweezers or anything that may push the object farther into the ear.

If the object is hard, like plastic or metal, then try to wash it out with warm water, just as for wax. Do not do this for vegetable objects like seeds, because they swell when they get wet and become more difficult to remove.

Stop if the object starts to move further into the ear or if your child cannot keep still. You could damage the ear canal or the ear drum.

INFECTION OF THE EAR CANAL CAUSED BY OBJECTS OR WATER IN THE EAR

Infection in the outer ear can be caused by insects, wax, water, or other material getting into the ear, or if a child scratches inside the ear with something (like a small stick). This infection of the ear canal is more common in adults than in children.

Signs:

- Pain — if wiggling the outer ear causes pain, there is probably infection in the outer ear.

- Itching in the ear

- A blocked or full feeling in the ear

- The ear canal may be swollen.

- A child may hear less well in the affected ear.

Prevention:

Older children can help care for their brothers' and sisters' ears by checking regularly to see if there is a lot of wax (or pus, or any objects) inside. Ask them to tell you right away if they see anything wrong.

Teach them never to put their fingers or anything else in the ear to try and remove objects or wax. This can push the material in farther and damage the ear drum. Prevent children from scratching inside the ear with anything, as it can cause infection.

Keep children's ears dry. After swimming or bathing, teach children to shake their heads gently to clear the water out. If possible, children should not swim or bathe in dirty or polluted water. If a child has had infections before, try putting a few drops of rubbing alcohol or vinegar into his ears after swimming or bathing.

For infection of the ear canal caused by objects or water in the ear

Mix 1 spoon of vinegar with 1 spoon of boiled water (cooled until warm). Put drops of this solution into the ear 3 or 4 times a day.

If there is fever or swelling around the ear:
give ampicillin, amoxicillin, or penicillin (same dosage as for sudden ear infection, see pages 195 to 196).

It is best to take the child to a hospital immediately. But if you cannot and if there is no improvement in 2 days then change to amoxicillin with cloxacillin (same dose as amoxicillin on page 195, but 4 times a day instead of 3), or erythromycin (see page 196 for dose). Use for 5 to 7 days.

If there is a lot of wax or anything else in the ear:
Wax can be removed by washing with warm water (see page 199). The ear must be kept as dry as possible afterward.

If infection or itching continues after the bad pain goes away:
put 2 or 3 drops of gentian violet (2% in 70% alcohol) in the ear once a week for 2 or 3 weeks.

Note: A child can bathe, but should not put his ears under water or swim for 2 weeks after the infection is gone.

Childhood illnesses

Infection during childhood by diseases such as malaria, measles, mumps, or meningitis can damage the hearing nerve. Sometimes only one ear is affected, but meningitis usually affects both ears. For more about these illnesses, see Hesperian's book *Where There Is No Doctor*.

Prevent childhood illnesses with immunizations

Immunize children against all the childhood diseases — especially those that can cause deafness, such as measles, mumps, and rubella (German measles). Vaccinations are usually given free. It is better to take your children to be immunized than to take them for treatment when they are sick or dying.

If health workers do not immunize in your village, take your children to the nearest health center to be immunized. Or work together with other people in your area to bring health workers to your community. Immunizations save lives and hearing — they should be made easily available.

Treatment for childhood illnesses

Children should stay in bed, drink lots of liquids, and eat nutritious food. If a baby cannot breastfeed, give breast milk in a spoon.

For fever
Give paracetamol (acetaminophen — see page 195).

If fluid starts draining from the ear
Give an antibiotic by mouth as for sudden infections (page 195).

If signs of chronic ear infection develop
See pages 196 to 197.

If the child has diarrhea
Give rehydration drink in small sips, 1 glass for each watery stool.

In 1 liter of clean water mix half a teaspoon of salt with 8 teaspoons of sugar. Or make a watery porridge with 1 liter of clean water, half a teaspoon of salt and 8 heaped teaspoons of powdered cereal (rice flour, maize flour, wheat flour, sorghum, or cooked and mashed potatoes).

If signs of pneumonia, meningitis, or severe pain in the ear or stomach develop, get medical help.

MEASLES

Measles causes ear infections in many children. Measles may damage the inner ear and also may cause a middle ear infection with an ear

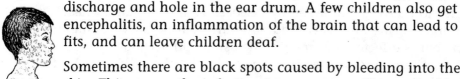

discharge and hole in the ear drum. A few children also get encephalitis, an inflammation of the brain that can lead to fits, and can leave children deaf.

Sometimes there are black spots caused by bleeding into the skin. This means the infection is very severe. Get medical help.

Prevention:

Children from other families should not go to a house where someone has measles. They should stay away from children with measles and their brothers and sisters. To prevent the illness from spreading, children in a family where someone has measles should not go to school, stores, markets, or other public places for 10 days, even if they are not sick themselves.

Children who are weak, poorly nourished, or who have tuberculosis or HIV/AIDS need to be carefully protected from measles. It is especially dangerous for them.

No school for you, Lan, until Thuy is all better.

MUMPS

Mumps infection begins with fever, and pain when opening
the mouth or eating. In 2 days, swelling develops on the side of
the neck. Sometimes mumps can cause severe hearing loss, usually
in only one ear. The swelling goes away after about 10 days, without
need for medicine. For pain or fever give paracetamol (acetaminophen).
Feed the child soft, nutritious foods and keep his mouth clean.
Get medical help if signs for meningitis appear (see page 204).

MALARIA

Children who are seriously ill with malaria can become deaf. Malaria
is an infection of the blood, spread by mosquitoes, that causes chills
and high fever (40°C or 104°F or more). Sometimes this deafness may
go away within 2 to 3 days. But children who have been sick with
malaria are weaker and get ear infections more easily, which can also
cause deafness.

To treat malaria

- In areas where malaria is common, treat any unexplained fever as malaria.

- When children have repeated fevers or if you suspect malaria, see
  a health worker, and if possible go to a health center for a blood
  test. In areas where an especially dangerous type of malaria
  called falciparum occurs, seek treatment immediately.

- If a child who may have malaria begins to have convulsions
  (fits) or other signs of meningitis (see the next page) he may
  have cerebral malaria. Get medical help immediately.

Note: The treatment for malaria is different in different places. Medicines
that work well in one place may not be effective in another place. Find out
from a health worker which malaria medicine works best in your area. Some
medicines used to treat malaria can also cause deafness (see page 206).

Prevention:

- Cover sleeping children, or use mosquito nets or a thin cloth over
  beds and cradles. Nets treated with insecticide work best.

- Reduce standing water, which is the breeding ground for the
  mosquitos that pass malaria. Clear away cans, pots, or old tires
  that collect water. Drain, fill, or release fish into pools of water, or
  marshes. Fill the tops of bamboo posts with sand.

- Prevent or reduce the effects by taking anti-malaria medicines.

If malaria is suspected, get treatment quickly. This will keep malaria
from being passed to others.

MENINGITIS

Meningitis (brain fever) is a serious infection of the brain that can spread to the ear nerves and cause deafness. Or ear infections can spread towards the brain and cause meningitis. Meningitis may begin after another childhood illness, such as measles, mumps, whooping cough, or an ear infection. It may also be caused by a virus.

Signs of meningitis:

The signs of meningitis are severe headache and fever. The child may be sleepy and have fits or jerks. Sometimes there is vomiting and a rash. A child with meningitis may faint (quickly go unconscious).

**Get medical help fast —
every minute counts.
Take the child to the hospital!**

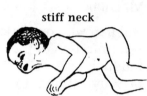

soft spot bulges up
(babies under 1 year)

stiff neck

back arched,
knees forward

To treat meningitis while taking the child to a hospital

Inject **one** of the following 3 medicines in the muscle or in the vein. Injections in the vein should be done only by a well-trained health worker. If a health worker is not available, it is best to inject the child in a muscle.

- ceftriaxone

  give 50 mg to 100 mg for every kilo of body weight, 1 time only

  or

- benzylpenicillin

  age less than 1 year .... 300 mg (500,000 units), 1 time only

  age 1 to 9 years .... 600 mg (1,000,000 units), 1 time only

  age 10 years or more .... 1.2 g (2,000,000 units), 1 time only

  or

- cefotaxime

  age less than 1 year .... 12.5 mg to 50 mg (for severe infection) per kilo of body weight, 4 times a day. (A 10 kg child needs at least 125 mg and up to 500 mg per dose.)

  age 1 to 9 years .... 25 to 50 mg per kilo of body weight, 4 times a day. (A 20 kg child needs at least 500 mg and up to 1000 mg per dose.)

Lower a high fever with wet cloths and/or paracetamol (see page 195).

If other medicines are not available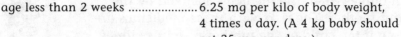
- give chloramphenicol by mouth, if possible. If not, by injection in the muscle or the vein, changing to by mouth as soon as possible.

  age less than 2 weeks .... 6.25 mg per kilo of body weight, 4 times a day. (A 4 kg baby should get 25 mg per dose.)

  age 2 weeks to 1 year of age .... 12.5 mg per kilo of body weight, 4 times a day. (A 10 kg child should get 125 mg per dose.)

  age 2 years or more .... 12.5 to 25 mg per kilo of body weight, 4 times a day. (A 10 kg child should get between 125 mg and 250 mg per dose.)

Note: Chloramphenicol should be used only for severe, life-threatening infections such as meningitis. In very severe cases chloramphenicol may be given as well as benzylpenicillin.

JAUNDICE

Sometimes a baby becomes yellow soon after birth. This is a sign of jaundice. If the baby is energetic and breastfeeding well, a little yellow color is normal between 2 and 5 days old — the mother should keep breastfeeding often and let the baby get plenty of sun. The jaundice may be more severe if the yellow color starts from the first day after birth, if it extends to the hands and feet, or if the baby is unusually sleepy and sucks poorly. **Get medical help.** Severe jaundice can be dangerous, and may also cause hearing loss.

HIV/AIDS

Children with HIV/AIDS have low resistance to infections. Their lower immunity leads to increased risk of infections such as cytomegalovirus (CMV), syphilis, tuberculosis (TB), and some types of meningitis. All these illnesses can damage the ear. See the book *HIV, Health, and Your Community*, published by the Hesperian Foundation, for ways to prevent HIV/AIDS.

Medicines that damage hearing

Some medicines can damage the hearing of children who take them. Several medicines can cause hearing loss in unborn babies when the medicine is taken by the pregnant mother. The risks with these medicines are increased if the child or the mother also has kidney disease. Some common medicines that damage hearing are:

- Some powerful antibiotics that contain aminoglycoside can cause deafness in children (such as amikacin, garamycin, gentamicin, kanamycin, neomycin, netilmicin, streptomycin, or tobramycin). This can happen when the child himself is given the antibiotic, or when his mother was given the medicine during pregnancy. These antibiotics usually have to be injected. They should be used only for serious infections that could cause death.

- Children under 12 should not take aspirin. For pain and fever children can take paracetamol (acetominophen). Aspirin can damage the hearing when taken at higher than normal doses. It can also cause temporary deafness and buzzing in the ear (tinnitus) but these usually stop soon after stopping the aspirin.

- Quinine and chloroquine (which are used to treat malaria) can both sometimes damage hearing in the person taking them.

- If a mother uses thalidomide in pregnancy (to treat cancer, leprosy, or conditions associated with HIV/AIDS), it can cause many severe defects in a baby, including hearing problems.

Traditional ear medicines

Traditional medicines and treatments are sometimes used to treat ear problems. Some traditional treatments can be harmful. Here are some general things to remember about traditional cures for health problems:

- Never use human or animal excrement as a cure. It can give the person an infection.

- The more the cure looks like or resembles the sickness, the more likely its effect comes only from people's belief in it.

- Ears are very fragile. Do not put anything very hot in or near the ear. It can also be dangerous to pour liquids or put things in the ear.

Prevention:

- Help mothers avoid using medicines during pregnancy that can cause deafness in children. Pregnant women should always consult a doctor or health worker before taking medicine during pregnancy.

*Let's see if we can find an antibiotic that is safe for you **and** your baby.*

- Tell a health worker immediately if you think a medicine is affecting hearing.

- Do not allow untrained people to inject antibiotics.

- Do not inject powerful antibiotics like gentamicin unless it is necessary to save a life and there are no other medicines available.

Women's health can damage or protect children's hearing

It is important that girls and women, especially pregnant women, have enough good food and access to health care. A baby can be born with hearing loss because:

- his mother was sick or did not eat well as a young girl, or during her pregnancy. For example, a baby born to a mother who did not get enough to eat can often be born early or have low birth weight and his hearing can be damaged.

- sickness or poor nutrition caused problems during birth. For example, if a woman has a small pelvis from poor nutrition, her baby may get stuck during birth. This could cause hearing loss from brain damage.

- some infections can pass from the mother to the baby during pregnancy and damage the baby's hearing. These infections include rubella (German measles), tuberculosis, cytomegalovirus (CMV), and syphilis.

LACK OF IODINE IN THE DIET DURING PREGNANCY

Iodine is a mineral found in the soil and water — and in foods like liver, onions, egg yolks, seafood, and plants from the ocean. When a pregnant woman does not get enough iodine, her baby may be born mentally slow, or have serious problems including deafness.

In some places in the world, the soil contains very little natural iodine so vegetables and crops that grow in the soil also contain little iodine. In these places, swelling of the thyroid gland in the neck is common. This is called goiter. If many people in your community have this swelling, then everyone needs more iodine.

goiter

A child with iodine deficiency may be mentally slow, deaf, unable to speak, and have weak neck and leg muscles. Many children only suffer hearing loss, some weakness in the legs, and are slow to learn. But others may have noses with a flat wide base, squinting eyes, hair low on the forehead, puffy eyelids and face, and have physical problems such as growing slowly and being short.

Treatment:

Get medical advice as soon as you can. A medicine called thyroxine, if started in the first months of life, may help a child with iodine deficiency grow better, though it will not help a child hear better.

The whole community, including the affected child, needs iodine supplements, but this will not help any nerve or brain damage that has already occurred.

Prevention:

Goiter and iodine deficiency are easy and cheap to prevent. Women must get iodine before becoming pregnant. Taking iodine after the first few weeks of pregnancy is too late.

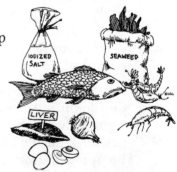

Foods from the ocean, as well as liver, egg yolks, and onions, can be good sources of iodine.

- The easiest way to get enough iodine is to use iodized salt instead of natural or rock salt. You can find packaged iodized salt in most places.

- Iodized oil taken by mouth is available in some countries. You need to take only 1 dose every 1 to 5 years.

- If iodized salt or iodine-rich foods are hard to get, you can make an iodine solution at home with Lugol's iodine. This is an antiseptic that is often available where medicines are sold.

To make an iodine solution to drink:
Add 1 drop of Lugol's iodine to 1 glass of clean drinking water
or milk. Drink this once a week. **Store iodine at room
temperature and in dark containers to protect it from light.**

RUBELLA (GERMAN MEASLES)

Rubella usually causes only a slight rash and gives the person no
other problems. But if a woman who is pregnant gets rubella
during the first 3 months of pregnancy, her child may
be born deaf or with other serious problems.

Prevention:

- Give rubella vaccination to girls before
  they are old enough to have babies. If
  vaccination is not available, let young girls
  build a resistance to rubella before they are old enough to have
  children. They can visit people in the community who have
  rubella. They may catch the infection and develop resistance.

- If girls and women have not been vaccinated or have not had
  rubella by the time they are old enough to have children, they
  should prevent deafness in their babies, if they are or might be
  pregnant, by staying away from people with rubella.

TUBERCULOSIS (TB)

Children of mothers who have tuberculosis during pregnancy
sometimes get a type of meningitis called 'tubercular meningitis' in
the first few months of life. This can cause deafness.

To treat tuberculosis
If anyone in the family might have tuberculosis, seek medical help and
see that the whole family is tested for TB. Begin treatment at once. Many
governments give the medicines for free. Early and full treatment is the
key to prevent the spread of TB. For more information on treating
tuberculosis see *Where There Is No Doctor* or another general health book.

Prevention:

- Immunize children against tuberculosis with the BCG vaccine.

- Everyone, especially children, should eat plenty of nutritious foods.

SYPHILIS

Syphilis is a sexually transmitted infection that can be passed from mother to baby during pregnancy and cause loss of hearing. Without treatment, syphilis can invade any part of the body. It can damage the inner ear and the nerves that affect hearing and cause deafness.

Signs:

The signs for syphilis in an infant or a child may be: rashes, blisters on the palms or toes, sores, or anal warts; swollen spleen, liver, or retina, or generalized swelling; jaundice, ringing in the ears, dizziness, deafness that comes and goes, loss of eyesight, and headaches. (Some of these signs are different from those in an adult.)

If there is any chance that someone, especially a pregnant woman or a child, may have syphilis, she should immediately see a health worker. Special blood tests and other tests may be needed. If the person cannot go to a health center or hospital, give the treatment for syphilis.

To treat syphilis (not neurosyphilis)

For children and adults who have had syphilis for less than 2 years:
- inject benzylpenicillin (also called penicillin G or crystalline penicillin) in the muscle. Give 1.2 million units (720 mg) in each buttock, 1 time only (a total dose of 2.4 million units or 1.44 g).

  (or)

- inject procaine benzylpenicillin in the muscle. Give 1.2 million units (1.2 g) every day, for 10 days.

For children and adults who have had syphilis for more than 2 years:
- inject benzylpenicillin in the muscle. Give 1.2 million units (720 mg) in each buttock, once a week for 3 weeks (2.4 million units per dose).

  (or)

- inject procaine benzylpenicillin in the muscle. Give 1.2 million units (1.2 g) every day for 3 weeks.

If allergic to penicillin and over 8 years old (and not pregnant)

For children and adults who have had syphilis for less than 2 years:
- give doxycycline, 2 mg for every kilo of body weight (to a maximum of 100 mg) by mouth, 2 times a day for 14 days.

For children and adults who have had syphilis for more than 2 years:
- give doxycycline, 4 mg for every kilo of body weight (to a maximum of 200 mg), by mouth, 2 times a day for 28 days.

WARNING: **Pregnant women must not use doxycycline.**

To treat neurosyphilis

When syphilis affects the nervous system it can cause severe hearing loss. This can happen when syphilis is left untreated, but babies can also be born with it. Fortunately this form of nerve deafness can be treated, which will prevent further hearing loss. Testing for neurosyphilis may include blood tests or a lumbar puncture (test of fluid from the spine). If you cannot get the child tested, but strongly suspect syphilis, give the treatment.

For children younger than 2 years:
• inject benzylpenicillin slowly into the muscle or into the vein.

  Give 25,000 units (15 mg) for every kilo of body weight 2 times a day for 10 days.

   or

• inject procaine benzylpenicillin slowly into the muscle.

  Give 50,000 units (50 mg) for every kilo of body weight 1 time a day for 10 days.

For children 2 years and older:
• inject benzylpenicillin slowly into the muscle or into the vein.

  Give 200,000 to 300,000 units (120 to 180 mg) for every kilo of body weight (up to a maximum of 2.4 million units or 1.44 g) 1 time a day for 14 days.

To cure syphilis completely, the full treatment is essential.

Hearing loss caused by syphilis may develop when the child is an infant, or later as a teenager. Treating syphilis will not fix any hearing loss that has already occurred, but it will prevent any hearing loss that could still be caused.

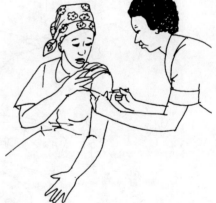

See the books **Where There Is No Doctor** or **Where Women Have No Doctor**, published by the Hesperian Foundation, for more information about syphilis.

Note: If a child has syphilis, the child's mother and her partner will also need treatment.

CYTOMEGALOVIRUS

Most people with cytomegalovirus (CMV) are not sick. But babies of mothers who become infected during pregnancy can have severe deafness, blindness, or physical and mental disability. The germs that spread CMV can be found in body fluids — like saliva, urine, stool, semen, vaginal fluids, and breast milk. To prevent the spread of CMV, wash hands with soap and water, especially after contact with stool, urine, or saliva.

BRAIN DAMAGE DURING BIRTH CAN CAUSE HEARING LOSS

If a baby suffers brain damage during labor or birth, he may be born deaf. The baby's brain can be damaged if there is not enough oxygen reaching it. This is more likely to happen if labor is very long, if the baby is in a difficult position for birth, or if there are twins.

To prevent brain damage during birth

Midwives and others caring for pregnant women can learn about the danger signs during pregnancy and labor when a woman must get medical help at a hospital. Community members can organize to make sure there are ways to get women to the hospital if there is an emergency.

- Some methods to make labor go faster can damage the baby's brain, which can cause deafness. To protect the baby, avoid these ways to make labor go faster:

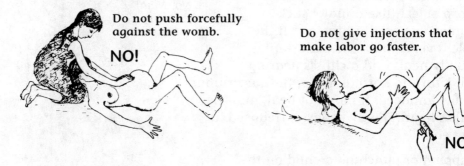

Do not push forcefully against the womb.

NO!

Do not give injections that make labor go faster.

NO!

- Get medical help right away if the labor is taking too long, if the baby is in a difficult position, or if the cord is around the baby's neck. For more information about safe birth, see **A Book for Midwives** published by the Hesperian Foundation.

Loud noises and injury can damage hearing

Some children lose their hearing because of very loud sounds or because of injury to their ears.

LOUD NOISES

Very loud noises — like bombs, gunfire, firecrackers, loud machinery, and loud music — can damage the inner ear and cause hearing loss. The amount of hearing loss depends on how loud the sound is, how long it lasts, and how often a child hears it. In countries affected by war, many children lose their hearing because of bombs, landmines, and gunfire. Noise damages the nerves in the inner ear. Explosions can damage the ear drum.

Prevention:

Try to keep your child away from loud noises as much as possible. If you cannot, try to protect his ears. Use something thick to cover his ears, like a thick blanket wrapped around his head, or thick ear muffs. You also need to protect your own ears from noise!

INJURY

A child can cause infection or poke a hole in the eardrum if she puts a sharp object (like a matchstick, feather, or pencil) in the ear. If the hole is very small, the ear drum usually heals and a child's hearing will return to normal. But if the ear drum is badly damaged, it may not heal, and the child's hearing may be lost or reduced in that ear.

No, Nina! Give me that!

Slapping or punching a child on the side of her head across her ear can burst her ear drum and cause deafness.

Head injuries with skull fractures can cause severe hearing loss. Bomb explosions and other very loud noises can burst the ear drums.

Prevention:

- Teach children not to put things in their ears.

- Never hit a child on the head, and work to reduce family violence.

War causes more and more childhood disability

We must all work to reduce the use of violence and war to solve political problems, and ban weapons that kill, disable, orphan, and make homeless thousands of children each year.

HEALTHCARE NOT WARFARE

SCHOOLS NOT BOMBS

PARENTS SAY NO TO WAR!

Hearing loss that is passed down in families

Some children's ears do not develop fully. This genetic problem is passed down in families — inherited from other family members and from earlier generations — although no one else in the family may show signs of deafness.

Grandfather was deaf, just like Lihua. I wonder how much deafness there has been in our family...

Hearing loss because of intermarriage

Some kinds of hearing loss can happen because of intermarriage between blood relatives, such as first cousins. In many village communities, intermarriage is common. Parents who are related to each other very closely can have children with hearing problems. If you, your children, or your family members have problems hearing, other children born later may also have hearing problems.

Sometimes a child who has an inherited hearing loss may also have other problems, such as problems seeing; different-colored eyes or white streaks in the hair; goiter or heart trouble; or abnormally-shaped bones of the head, hands, feet, arms, legs, or neck. But sometimes the only inherited problem is the hearing loss. Deafness may be partial or full, and may be from the time of birth, or may develop later.

Prevention:

Avoid marriage between blood relatives such as cousins. Genetic counselors (people who know about the risk of certain diseases being passed from parents to their children) are available in some cities. Try to talk to a health worker if you are concerned about hearing loss in your family.

This is my son Pratap. He is deaf, and so is my uncle.

Will our other babies be born deaf, too?

Working for change

Ruk's story

When Ruk was born in a village in Nepal, his mother struggled a long time to give birth. At first she thought her baby would not breathe. As a baby, Ruk would cry at night and he always seemed to have a cold or fever.

Ruk played on the mud floor and outside the house where his family spread the millet and corn to dry and separated the rice grain from the chaff and dust. Chickens, goats, and their dog lived in the same small area. Ruk loved to sit and watch his mother cook at the open stove, even though the wood smoke stung his eyes and made his nose run.

As Ruk grew older, he always seemed to have a runny nose. Sometimes he had very painful earaches in both ears, which often drained pus. He loved to swim in the small river below the village, but this made the pus drain even more.

When Ruk started going to school, he was slow to learn and not very good at reading. The teacher got angry because he thought Ruk was ignoring what he said. But it was hard for Ruk to hear the teacher. So, to avoid getting into trouble, Ruk sat at the back of the class. Children teased him. He spoke in a funny way and was difficult to understand.

Finally Ruk's parents decided it was not worth spending money to pay for his school uniform, books, and pens if he was not going to learn. So Ruk stopped going to school. Instead, he carried wood for the fire, fed the animals, and scrubbed the cooking pots for his mother.

One day, Ruk got a terrible earache that lasted for several days. His ear filled with pus and he developed a swelling behind the ear. Finally his father took him to the village herbal healer, but the medicines did not take away the swelling. His father had to carry Ruk to the health post in another village. The health worker there drained an abscess behind Ruk's ear and gave him an injection and some antibiotic syrup to take for a week.

After some time, Ruk had severe pain again. Both his ears always smelled bad and lots of pus came out of them. His neck got swollen and he had very high fever. The health worker told them to take Ruk to the hospital in the city. Ruk's parents had little money and did not know where they would stay, but they followed the health worker's advice.

Ruk almost died because the infection got into his brain and bloodstream. At the hospital, they gave him a lot of medicines but he was still very ill. Luckily, a visiting ear doctor drained the pus from the abscess, removed a lot of infected bone, and repaired his ear drum. The doctor explained how to take care of Ruk's ears and said Ruk should use a hearing aid. Ruk's parents just looked at the doctor and nodded.

Sandra, why do you think Ruk lost his hearing?

Maybe he lost some hearing during his difficult birth.

He had many fevers and colds. And his family didn't know that ear infections could damage his hearing.

There was no health worker nearby to tell them what to do.

I'll bet the smoke and the dust made his nose run and made his ear worse!

WHY DID RUK STOP GOING TO SCHOOL?

Ruk had really wanted to go to school and learn like the other children. Children who lose their hearing become disabled when teachers, family, and friends do not know how to communicate with them. If the school and the teacher knew that Ruk could not hear well they might have tried to communicate differently with him. They might even have helped other children understand that ear infections can cause children to lose their hearing. If the school had accepted Ruk and helped him to learn, he would have made friends and had a better future.

PEOPLE CAN CHANGE THE CONDITIONS THAT MAKE CHILDREN LOSE THEIR HEARING

Ruk's parents should have visited the health worker before he lost his hearing.

Yes, but if the health worker had come to the village and taught everyone the causes of deafness, they would have known what to do.

If we could grow more vegetables to eat, the children might not get sick so much.

And if the medicines were cheaper, they might have gotten them sooner.

Maybe the village could organize a way to get sick children to the hospital easily when they need it.

There is power in communities working for change. Here are some examples:

- People can organize local or national immunization campaigns against common childhood illnesses. Health workers can use simple health education materials with parents, children, teachers, and others.

- Health workers, teachers, and child care workers can be trained to recognize, treat, and prevent chronic ear infections and other causes of hearing loss in children.

- People can demand that the government make affordable medicines available to treat childhood illnesses, including ear infections, and that pharmacies and clinics in their communities keep them in stock.

- People can also work together to remove the communication barriers that make deafness a disability. They can learn sign language themselves, and they can work to provide educational opportunities for children who cannot hear well.

Improving the well-being of the whole community will help prevent and heal many of the problems that cause hearing loss. When a country's wealth is shared for the good of all its people, everyone — men and women, mothers and children — can have adequate health care, good roads and communication to receive medical attention when needed, and enough good food and clean water to help them grow strong and stay healthy.

Appendix A

Hearing aids

A hearing aid is a small piece of equipment that makes sounds louder. Many people think that a hearing aid will cure a child's hearing problem and make him hear sounds like other people do. This is not true. Hearing aids only make sounds louder. They do not fix any other problem. For more about different kinds of hearing loss, see Chapter 5, starting on page 47.

Hearing aids can be worn in one or both ears, depending on the kind of hearing loss a child has. They can help a child who hears some sounds to hear sounds better. If a child cannot hear **any** sounds, a hearing aid will probably not help.

Is a hearing aid right for my child?

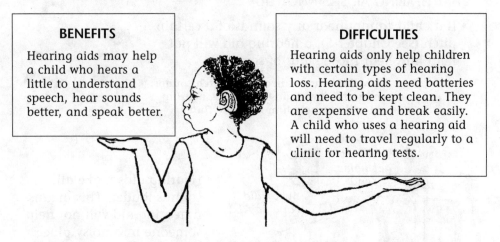

BENEFITS

Hearing aids may help a child who hears a little to understand speech, hear sounds better, and speak better.

DIFFICULTIES

Hearing aids only help children with certain types of hearing loss. Hearing aids need batteries and need to be kept clean. They are expensive and break easily. A child who uses a hearing aid will need to travel regularly to a clinic for hearing tests.

A hearing aid will only work well if it fits a child's ear exactly. The earmold (the part that fits in the ear) is made from impressions of the outer ear, and no two ears are the same. In young children, the earmold must be checked at least twice a year. It must be replaced as a child's ear grows and changes shape.

WHAT HEARING AIDS CAN DO

The benefits of a hearing aid depend on the kind of hearing loss a child has.

- If a child can hear some sounds, a hearing aid will help her hear sounds that are too soft for her to hear by herself.

- If a child can hear faint speech sounds, a hearing aid will make speech louder, and may help her hear what others say. This can also help a child learn to speak.

- If a child can hear some sounds, a hearing aid may alert him to sounds that warn about danger.

WHAT HEARING AIDS CANNOT DO

- If a child cannot hear any sounds of a certain pitch (see Chapter 5), a hearing aid will not help him hear those kinds of sounds.

This child cannot hear high-pitch sounds, no matter how loud they are. A hearing aid will not help him hear the flute.

We'd better get home, Yena.

What did Papa say?!

- Hearing aids make all sounds louder. This means a hearing aid will not help someone in a noisy place hear people more clearly than other noises.

Types of hearing aids

Here are 2 of the most common hearing aids that children use:

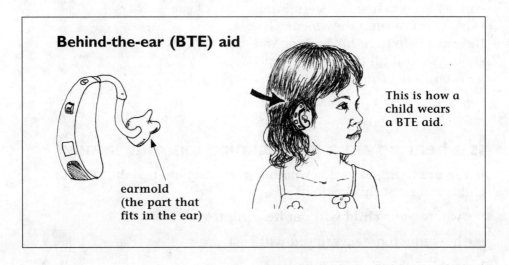

Behind-the-ear (BTE) aid

earmold
(the part that
fits in the ear)

This is how a
child wears
a BTE aid.

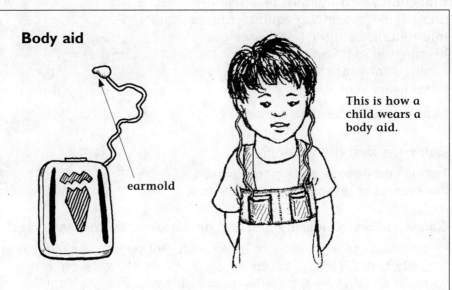

Body aid

earmold

This is how a
child wears a
body aid.

At one school for deaf children in India, all children wear
the hearing aids in a harness on the chest. The harness is
on the chest so the microphones can help the child hear his
own voice. The harness is made of thick cotton cloth, to
reduce noise from cloth. The microphones of the hearing
aid are kept in pockets. These pockets are tight (to reduce
cloth noise) and they keep the microphone visible.

If a child can use a hearing aid, it is best for the child to begin wearing the aid as soon as possible. This way he can get used to hearing sounds and start learning what they mean. To get the most help from his hearing aid, he should wear it all the time, except when he is bathing or sleeping.

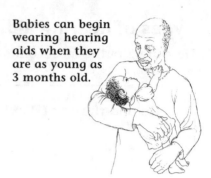
Babies can begin wearing hearing aids when they are as young as 3 months old.

Is a hearing aid a good choice for your family?

If you are trying to decide whether a hearing aid is right for your child, you must think about:

- **where your child will get hearing tests**
- **how much a hearing aid will cost**

Your child's hearing must be tested by someone who is trained and has testing equipment (see Chapter 5). Information from the test is used to set the hearing aid so it will make sounds the right loudness for your child. He will need to be tested every year.

Here are some questions to consider:

Can we afford the testing?

Testing can be expensive. Some places, however, offer testing free or at low cost.

Can we afford a hearing aid, and new earmolds and batteries?

Hearing aids are expensive to begin with, but buying the aid is not the only cost. A child between the ages of 2 and 6 will need a new earmold about every 6 months because his ears are growing fast. The earmold **must** fit well, otherwise the hearing aid will not work correctly.

Getting new earmolds and batteries can be very costly.

In some places, the government may have programs to give free or low-cost hearing aids to all children who need them. Try contacting the Ministry of Education, the Ministry of Health, or a school for the deaf. But such programs are not available everywhere.

You may need new batteries every week or every couple of months. How often you need new batteries depends on how many hours each day your child wears his hearing aid, the type of hearing aid he has, and the kind of batteries he uses. Some countries provide them free.

Hearing aids and batteries should be available to all children who can benefit from them, not just to families who can afford them!

Can we check the hearing aid every day and take care of it?

Oh no, I got wet.

Hearing aids need to be checked every morning to make sure the batteries and the aid are working well. The earmolds also need to be washed and dried regularly so that dirt will not block sound from getting to the ear.

And hearing aids must be handled carefully. If the aid gets wet, or is dropped, it may break or need repair.

If you decide to get a hearing aid

If you decide a hearing aid is right for your child, be sure that you receive information along with the aid so you can learn:

- how to help your child get used to wearing a hearing aid
- how to care for the hearing aid
- how to check the aid each day to be sure it is working
- what to do when the aid does not work well

▶ Ways to help your child get used to wearing a hearing aid

Every child reacts differently to wearing hearing aids. Some children like them right away, some children find them uncomfortable at first. At first, put the hearing aid on for only 15 to 30 minutes. Gradually increase the amount of time your child wears the aid. It may take many weeks for him to get used to wearing it.

If your child wears the hearing aid while he is enjoying himself, it is less likely to bother him.

Start using the hearing aid in a quiet environment to help your child become aware of the new sounds she can hear. Help her notice sounds by bringing your child closer to the sound or point the sound out to her.

You didn't know that washing dishes makes sounds, did you?

▶ How to know if your child is hearing new sounds

Do not expect your child to react to sounds immediately. Your child will have to learn to be aware of sounds after his hearing aid is put on. Children's reaction to sound depends on their age and how much they can hear.

You may have to watch carefully to see your child's reactions. She may:

- blink her eyes or stop what she is doing.
- enjoy playing with toys that make noise.
- cry when she hears a sound.
- look up or turn around when she hears a sound.

It may be weeks or months before you see your child react to sound.

Tuan Jai doesn't seem to be hearing anything. She doesn't look at the spoon when I tap it on the bowl.

▶ Help your child understand the new sounds she is hearing

Sonal, I know there is a lot of noise, but try to hear Mr. Murthy talking to you.

Even if a hearing aid helps your child hear sounds, she may not understand the sounds she is hearing right away. Your child will need practice listening to sounds with the hearing aid. See Chapter 6 for activities to help your child listen.

At first, she may find it uncomfortable to hear sounds, because she is used to living in a quieter world.

How to take care of hearing aids

With regular care, hearing aids will last longer, and give good sound.

Here are some tips to get better service from a hearing aid

• Keep the hearing aid far away from electrical equipment such as refrigerators and televisions.

• Do not let it get very hot or very cold.

• Keep it dry — sweat or water will damage it. During the day, remove it and wipe off any sweat or moisture. Remove the hearing aid before bathing, swimming, or when out in the rain. At night, put the hearing aid in a container with silica gel (a material that absorbs moisture). Do not use perfumes or any sort of spray on the hearing aid.

Cleaning

• Use a soft dry cloth to clean it. Never use any cleaning fluid.

Now let's rub it with the cloth.

Earmold

• Check for wax in the earmold regularly.

• Clean the ear mold with warm water.

Battery

• To make the battery last longer, turn the hearing aid off when it is not being used.

• Keep the battery clean, and remove it when the hearing aid is not being used for a length of time — for example, when a child sleeps at night.

• Change the battery regularly. To check if it is time to change the battery, turn the sound to the highest setting. If whistling is heard, the battery is okay. If not, it is time to get a new battery. If the battery loses power faster than usual, it may be a sign of a problem with the hearing aid.

• Store batteries in a cool, dry place. Bring a battery that has been kept in the refrigerator to room temperature before using.

Try to have the hearing aid checked at a hearing aid clinic or store periodically.

Hearing aids may need repair. Usually hearing aid repair can be done only in big cities. But deaf organizations have started training deaf people to take ear impressions, to make earmolds, and to repair hearing aids.

Common problems and solutions for hearing aids

Use this list to help you to check and fix some common problems with hearing aids. If the hearing aid still does not work, it may need to be repaired.

If the hearing aid is 'dead'

➤ Is it turned on? .... Switch on.

➤ Is the battery dead or weak? .... Replace battery.

➤ Is the battery inserted properly? .... Check that **+** and **–** signs on battery match those on hearing aid.

➤ Is the cord broken? .... Replace cord.

➤ Is the ear mold blocked? .... Clean blockage in ear mold.

➤ Did water get into the hearing aid? .... Remove battery, wipe clean, and put in case with silica gel.

If the sound is not loud enough

➤ Is the battery low? .... Replace battery.

➤ Is the sound set too low? .... Turn sound louder.

➤ Are the ear molds loose? .... Insert carefully.

➤ Is the ear mold blocked? .... Clean blockage in ear mold.

➤ Is there lots of ear wax in the ear? .... Clean ear wax (see page 199).

➤ Did the child's hearing change? .... Check hearing.

If bothersome noises come and go

➤ Is the battery low? .... Replace battery.

➤ Is the cord broken? .... Replace cord.

If there is a 'frying' noise

➤ Is the battery low? .... Replace battery.

If the sound is not clear, or is distorted

➤ Is the battery low? .... Replace battery.

➤ Is the cord broken? .... Replace cord.

➤ Is the microphone covered by clothes? ..... Expose microphone.

➤ Is the microphone covered with dust? ...... Clean with soft cloth or brush.

Appendix B
Cochlear implants and hearing

People are able to hear sounds because a part of the ear called the 'cochlea' sends signals about sound to the brain. If a person's cochlea is damaged, he will not be able to hear well.

A cochlear implant operation is a new way to help deaf children hear sound. Though it is very expensive, this operation is now available in many countries.

To give someone an 'artificial cochlea', the bones of his head must be cut open in an operation. A small piece of equipment called a 'cochlear implant' is inserted inside the innermost part of the ear.

the inside of the ear

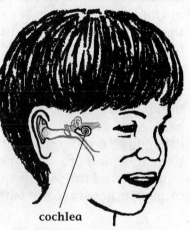

cochlea

The cochlea is a small part of the ear inside the head. It is shaped like a snail's shell.

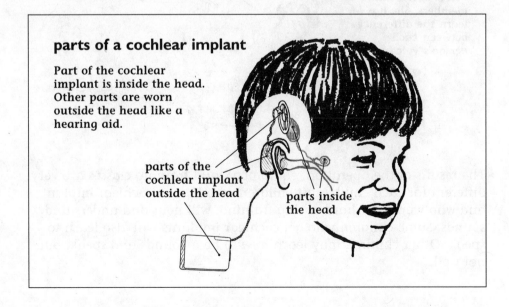

parts of a cochlear implant

Part of the cochlear implant is inside the head. Other parts are worn outside the head like a hearing aid.

parts of the cochlear implant outside the head

parts inside the head

Who can be helped by a cochlear implant?

The cochlear implant is only given to children who are completely deaf or have very little hearing even with a hearing aid. In some countries, babies as young as 6 months can get cochlear implants. In other places they must be 1 to 2 years old. Cochlear implants do not help people who already have some hearing.

Effect of cochlear implant on hearing

Cochlear implants do not cure deafness. The implant's outside microphone and processor send signals to the implant which passes them to the brain. The outside parts are tuned over a period of time to meet each child's needs.

If your child does not use the cochlear implant correctly, he will not hear any sounds. Even when cochlear implants work well, hearing through an implant sounds different from normal hearing. Some people say that sounds seem flat or 'tinny' — they compare it to listening to a radio station that does not come in clearly. It will take some time and practice for children with cochlear implants to learn to understand the sounds they hear. Children must go to classes to be trained in how to 'hear' with the cochlear implant.

This child can hear the voices of her family members. She has to learn the difference between each person's voice.

Who's talking now, Nami?

The results of the operation, equipment, and training classes are very different for each child. Most children who have a cochlear implant, and who work very hard during training, will hear and understand sounds. Some children who get cochlear implants will also learn to speak. Other children may learn how to hear sounds and speak, but not well.

Is a cochlear implant a good choice for your family?

If you are trying to decide whether a cochlear implant is a reasonable choice for your child, here are some things to consider.

ARE COCHLEAR IMPLANTS AND PROFESSIONAL SUPPORT AVAILABLE IN YOUR AREA?

Many communities do not have doctors or professionals who are trained to work with cochlear implants. Most countries have some doctors who can perform the operation, but they are usually in big city hospitals where there may also be a cochlear implant center.

Having a cochlear implant center near you is important. You and your child will visit the center many times for several years. Your Ministry of Health or a school for the deaf might be able to tell you if there is a cochlear implant center close to you.

COST OF THE OPERATION AND COCHLEAR IMPLANT

The operation, equipment, and years of training with professionals are very expensive. In India, cochlear implants can cost about $10,000. (Hearing aids cost about $75.) As with hearing aids, children can lose or break parts that are worn outside the head. These parts can be very expensive to replace.

In China, the operation, equipment, and training equals 20 years of an average worker's salary.

In Mexico, the cost of a cochlear implant equals 4 years of a medical doctor's salary.

Older and cheaper cochlear implants do not work as well as the newer, more expensive equipment. In a few countries, programs offer the cochlear implant for free or at low cost.

Cochlear implants, like other kinds of health care, should not only be given to those who are rich enough to afford them. If a cochlear implant is the best thing for a child, the operation and support should be made available.

Cochlear implants and illness

Sometimes the cochlear implant can cause ear infections that can make hearing worse. It is important to treat ear infections quickly in children who have cochlear implants. It is also important to vaccinate them against childhood illness.

The cochlear implant equipment and operation can also cause a serious illness called meningitis, even years later. Meningitis is a very serious infection of the brain and can happen more in children who:

- are younger than 5 years old.

- became deaf because of meningitis.

- have ear infections.

- get sick often.

For more information about meningitis, see page 201, as well as the book *Where There Is No Doctor*, published by the Hesperian Foundation.

CARE AND SUPPORT AFTER THE OPERATION

Young children with a cochlear implant need extra care and help from their families and professionals. After children heal from the operation, they must spend years training with professionals to learn to hear and to understand the sounds they hear. The family will also need training in how to communicate with the child.

Say 'apple'.

Abba.

Appendix C
Child development charts

How to use these child development charts

Children develop in several main areas: **physical** (the body), **mental** (the mind), **communication** (signing or talking), and **social** (relating to other people). Any one action a child does often includes a skill from each area. For example, when a child reaches his arms up to be held, he is using a:

- physical skill — he holds up his arms
- mental skill — he recognizes you
- communication skill — he tells you what he wants
- social skill — he enjoys being held by you

The charts in this chapter show some of the skills children learn and the age at which most children learn them. You can use the charts to get general information about how children develop and to help you decide what skills your child needs to learn.

| 6 | 12 | 2 |
| months | months | years |

The charts show how children's physical skills change as children grow.

▶ *How to know what skills your child needs to learn*

Find the chart for the age group closest to your child's age. On the chart, circle the skills your child has. You may find your child does not have some skills that other children his age have. Knowing this can help you decide which activities you want to work on with your child.

If your child's development is behind others his age

It is important to work on the skills your child needs to learn **next**, even if they are skills that other children usually learn much earlier. When your child has mastered more basic skills, he will be able to learn skills that others his age are learning. Trying to teach a child skills before he is ready will lead to frustration for both you and your child.

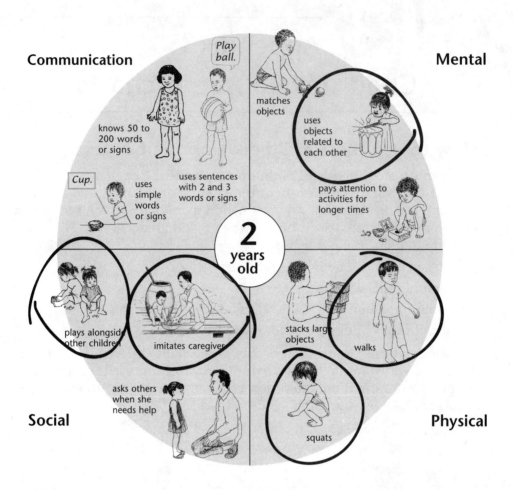

Communication

matches objects

Play ball.

knows 50 to 200 words or signs

Cup.

uses simple words or signs

uses sentences with 2 and 3 words or signs

Mental

uses objects related to each other

pays attention to activities for longer times

2 years old

Social

plays alongside other children

imitates caregiver

asks others when she needs help

stacks large objects

walks

squats

Physical

In the chart above, a mother has circled the skills her 20-month-old daughter can do. Her child needs help to gain skills in each area, but most of all she needs help in the communication area and in the mental area. For a child this young, the family should be working on basic communication (Chapter 4) and beginning to introduce language.

For an older child, you can start by looking at the chart that is nearest his age. But you may have to look at the charts for younger children to see the skills the child can do. Other charts will give you an idea of the kinds of skills your child will need to learn before he can work on learning skills like the ones on the chart nearest his age.

If your child cannot hear well, it is likely that he needs extra help to develop his communication, mental, and social skills. Chapters 2 and 3 will be helpful because they explain how children learn language and give some general tips for how to work with young children. Because children's mental skills grow together with their communication skills, the activities in Chapters 4, 7, 8, and 9 will help a child increase both his communication and mental development. Chapter 12, on social skills, suggests many ways you can help a child develop his social interactions.

Each part of this circle shows a different area of development. The pictures and words are examples of skills that many babies have when they are **3 months old.**

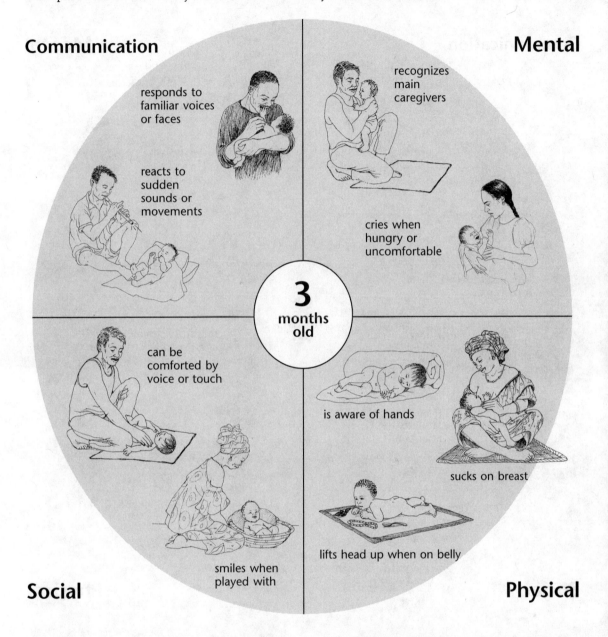

Communication

responds to familiar voices or faces

reacts to sudden sounds or movements

Mental

recognizes main caregivers

cries when hungry or uncomfortable

3 months old

can be comforted by voice or touch

is aware of hands

sucks on breast

smiles when played with

lifts head up when on belly

Social

Physical

Babies who are deaf or cannot hear well will benefit from activities that help them develop in all of the skills in each area. The pictures are only **examples** of skills. In this example, look at the 'Communication' part of the circle: You do not have to play the flute! The question to ask yourself is if your baby reacts to a sudden sound or movement.

Keep in mind that the goal is for your baby to do the activities that other babies the same age do in your community.

Each part of this circle shows a different area of development. The pictures and words are examples of skills that many babies have when they are **6 months old**.

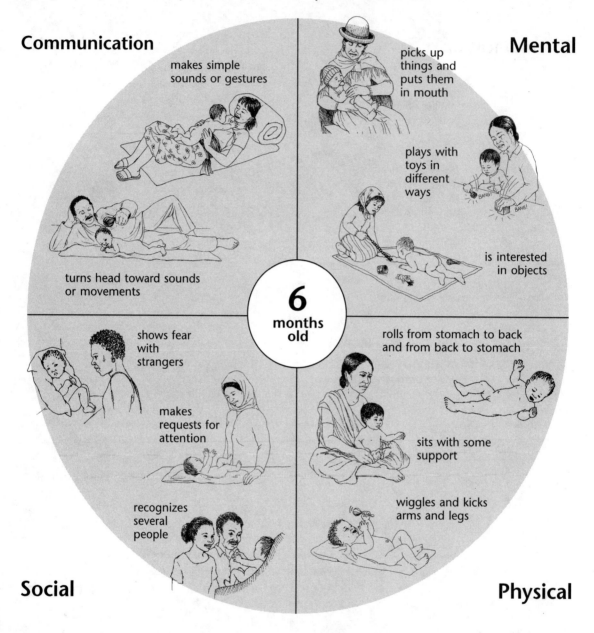

Communication

makes simple sounds or gestures

turns head toward sounds or movements

Mental

picks up things and puts them in mouth

plays with toys in different ways

is interested in objects

6 months old

Social

shows fear with strangers

makes requests for attention

recognizes several people

Physical

rolls from stomach to back and from back to stomach

sits with some support

wiggles and kicks arms and legs

Babies who are deaf or cannot hear well will benefit from activities that help them develop in all of the skills in each area. The pictures are only **examples** of skills. In this example, look at the 'Physical' part of the circle: Your baby does not have to play with a rattle. The question to ask yourself is if your baby wiggles and kicks.

Keep in mind that the goal is for your baby to do the activities that other babies the same age do in your community.

Each part of this circle shows a different area of development. The pictures and words are examples of skills that many babies have when they are **12 months old.**

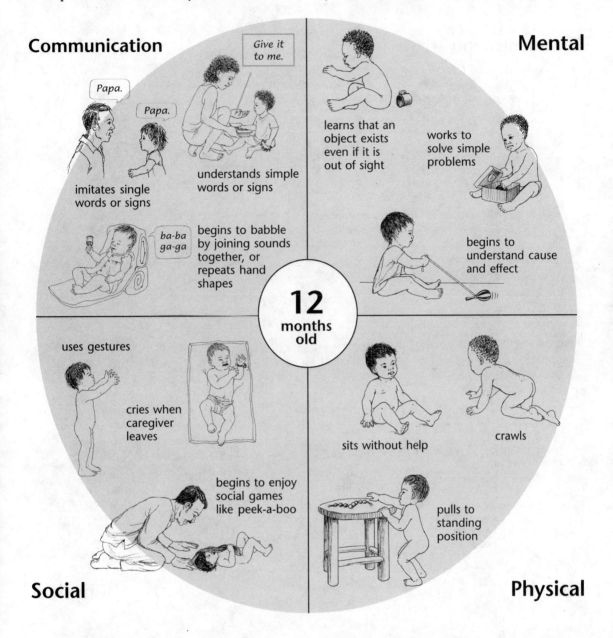

Communication

imitates single words or signs

Papa.

Papa.

Give it to me.

understands simple words or signs

ba-ba ga-ga

begins to babble by joining sounds together, or repeats hand shapes

Mental

learns that an object exists even if it is out of sight

works to solve simple problems

begins to understand cause and effect

12 months old

Social

uses gestures

cries when caregiver leaves

begins to enjoy social games like peek-a-boo

Physical

sits without help

crawls

pulls to standing position

Babies who are deaf or cannot hear well will benefit from activities that help them develop in all of the skills in each area. The pictures are only **examples** of skills. In this example, look at the 'Social' part of the circle: You do not have to play peek-a-boo with your baby. The question to ask yourself is if your baby enjoys social games.

Keep in mind that the goal is for your baby to do the activities that other babies the same age do in your community.

Each part of this circle shows a different area of development. The pictures and words are examples of skills that many children have when they are **2 years old**.

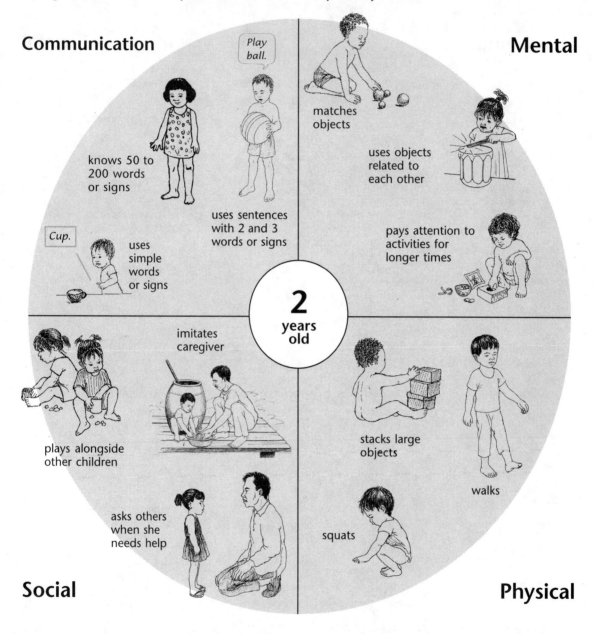

Children who are deaf or cannot hear well will benefit from activities that help them develop in all of the skills in each area. The pictures are only **examples** of skills. In this example, look at the 'Mental' part of the circle: Your child does not have to be able to play a drum. The question to ask yourself is if your child uses 2 objects together.

Keep in mind that the goal is for your child to do the activities that other children the same age do in your community.

Each part of this circle shows a different area of development. The pictures and words are examples of skills that many children have when they are **3 years old.**

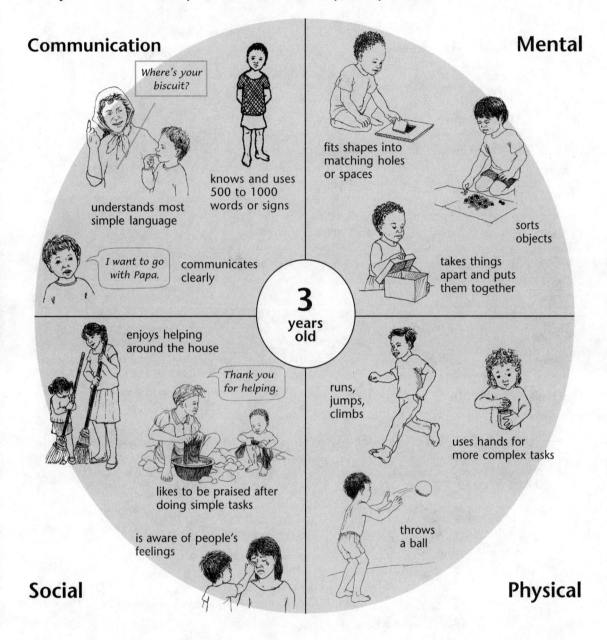

Children who are deaf or cannot hear well will benefit from activities that help them develop in all of the skills in each area. The pictures are only **examples** of skills. In this example, look at the 'Social' part of the circle: Your child does not have to sweep the floor. The question to ask yourself is if your child enjoys helping work with the family.

Keep in mind that the goal is for your child to do the activities that other children the same age do in your community.

Each part of this circle shows a different area of development. The pictures and words are examples of skills that many children have when they are **5 years old**.

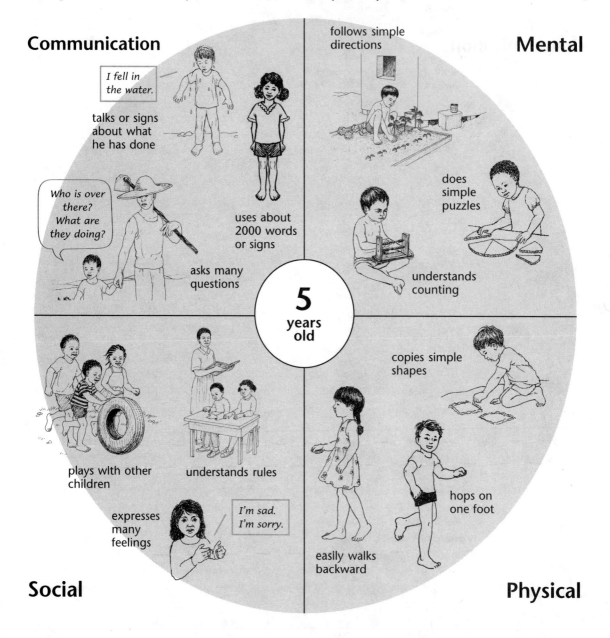

Communication

I fell in the water.

talks or signs about what he has done

Who is over there? What are they doing?

uses about 2000 words or signs

asks many questions

Mental

follows simple directions

does simple puzzles

understands counting

5 years old

copies simple shapes

hops on one foot

Physical

easily walks backward

understands rules

I'm sad. I'm sorry.

plays with other children

expresses many feelings

Social

Children who are deaf or cannot hear well will benefit from activities that help them develop in all of the skills in each area. The pictures are only **examples** of skills. In this example, look at the 'Social' part of the circle: Your child does not have to be paying attention to a teacher. The question to ask yourself is if your child understands rules like other children do.

Keep in mind that the goal is for your child to do the activities that other children the same age do in your community.

Where to get more information

Here is a small selection of organizations and printed materials that can provide useful information about deafness and young children. We have tried to list organizations and materials covering as many of the topics in this book as possible, and to include groups working in all areas of the world. Many of the printed materials are easy to adapt and often include other helpful resource lists.

ORGANIZATIONS

Alexander Graham Bell Association for the Deaf and Hard of Hearing (AG Bell)
3417 Volta Place, NW
Washington, DC 20007
USA
phone: (1-202) 337-5220
tty: (1-202) 337-5221
fax: (1-202) 337-8314
website: www.agbell.org

AG Bell offers its members a wide range of programs and services about hearing loss, resources, and support and encouragement from people who know and understand deaf issues and needs. AG Bell publishes and distributes books, brochures, instructional materials, videos, CDs, and audiocassettes related to hearing loss.

Ali Yavar Jung National Institute for the Hearing Handicapped
K.C. Marg
Bandra Reclamation, Bandra (W)
Mumbai 400 050
India
phone: (91-22) 2640-0215, 2645-5937
fax: (91-22) 2642-2638
email: ido@ayjnihh.org
website: www.ayjnihh.org

Collects and shares information about deafness, offers training, and develops strategies for early identification, intervention, and rehabilitation services. Source for teaching aids, films, and audio visuals on vocational training, job placement, and other issues.

Christian Blind Mission International (CBMI)
Nibelungenstrasse 124
D-64625 Bensheim
Germany
phone: (49-6251) 131-215
fax: (49-6251) 131-165
email: cbm_bensheim@compuserve.com
website: www.cbmi.org

The Christoffel Blindenmission International (CBMI) works to prevent blindness and supports medical, educational, and community-based rehabilitation activities for disabled persons. They also offer support to deaf and hard-of-hearing people.

Deaf Africa Fund (DAF)
Chapel Cottage, 7 King Street
Much Wenlock
Shropshire TF13 6BL
United Kingdom
phone: (44-1952) 727- 093
fax: (44-1952) 728- 473
email: dewdaf@aol.com

Promotes educational opportunities for deaf children in poor countries.

Delhi Foundation of Deaf Women

First Floor, DDA Community Hall
Gali Chandiwali, Pahar Ganj
New Delhi 110 055
India
phone: (91-11) 2353-3276
fax: (91-11) 2353-3276
email: info@dfdw.org
website: www.dfdw.org

*This organization helps deaf women
help themselves.*

**Disabled Children's Action Group
(DICAG) South Africa**

3rd Floor, Norlen House
17 Buitenkant Street
Cape Town 8001
South Africa
email: dicag@iafrica.com

*DICAG is a campaigning organization that
helps to raise the level of awareness of
disability and challenges stereotypes and
perceptions of disabled people in South Africa.
DICAG aims to ensure equal opportunities for
disabled children, especially in education.*

Enabling Education Network (EENET)

c/o Educational Support and Inclusion,
School of Education
University of Manchester, Oxford Road
Manchester M13 9PL
United Kingdom
phone: (44-161) 275-3711
fax: (44-161) 275-3548
email: info@eenet.org.uk
website: www.eenet.org.uk

*This information-sharing network promotes
inclusion of marginalized groups in
education. They produce a regular newsletter
which publishes case studies of exciting
programs worldwide and includes
contributions of parents' groups. They offer
many useful English
language publications.
The website has a
section dedicated to
deaf issues.*

The Forest Bookshop

Unit 2, New Building
Ellwood Road
Milkwall, Coleford
Glos. GL16 7LE
United Kingdom
phone: (44-1594) 833-858
fax: (44-1594) 833-446
website: www.forestbooks.com

*A comprehensive resource for books, videos,
and CD-ROMs on deafness and deaf issues.
Also distributes books published by
Gallaudet University.*

Gallaudet University

800 Florida Avenue, NE
Washington, DC 20002-3695
USA
phone/tty: (1-202) 651-5000
email: visitors.center@gallaudet.edu
website: www.gallaudet.edu

*Gallaudet University is the only liberal arts
university in the world designed exclusively
for deaf and hard-of-hearing students. It is
also an excellent source for finding deaf
books, journals, and current research.*

**International Deaf Children's Society
(IDCS)**

15 Dufferin Street
London EC1Y 8UR
United Kingdom
phone: (44-020) 7490-8656
fax: (44-020) 7251-5020
email: idcs@idcs.info
website: www.idcs.info

*An organization of families and caregivers
of deaf children, as well as the organizations
and professionals who work with them.
Established to share information and
experiences, IDCS provides a forum for
ideas, discussion, research and
information on all aspects of
childhood deafness on a global scale.*

Royal National Institute for the Deaf (RNID)
19-23 Featherstone Street
London EC1Y 8SL
United Kingdom
phone: (44-171) 296-8000
fax: (44-171) 296-8199
website: www.rnid.org.uk

The RNID has many online publications and useful links, as well as a large library database with detailed information about resources for people who are deaf. They also have a training and information resource called Deaf at Birth (website: www.deafnessatbirth.org.uk).

World Federation of the Deaf (WFD)
PO Box 65
00401 Helsinki
Finland
tty: (358-9) 580- 3573
fax: (358-9) 580-3572
email: info@wfdnews.org
website: www.wfdnews.org

One of the oldest international organizations of deaf people, WFD includes national organizations of deaf people in 120 countries. WFD works for human rights and equal opportunity for deaf people, and the right of deaf people to use sign language to get education and information. WFD initiated the annual Deaf Awareness Week to celebrate the culture, heritage, and language unique to deaf people of the world.

PRINTED MATERIALS

Choices in Deafness: A parent's guide to communication options (1996, 275 pages)
Sue Schwartz
   Woodbine House
   6510 Bells Mill Rd
   Bethesda, MD 20817, USA
   phone inside the US: (1-800) 843-7323
   phone outside the US: (1-301) 897-3570
   fax: (1-301) 897-5838
   website: www.woodbinehouse.com

Explanations of hearing loss followed by parents discussing why and how they made their choices among different approaches to communication.

The Deaf Child in the Family and at School: Essays in honor of Kathryn P. Meadows-Orlans (2000, 336 pages)
P.E. Spencer, C.J. Erting, and M. Marschark
   Lawrence Erlbaum Associates
   10 Industrial Avenue
   Mahwah, NJ 07430-2262, USA
   phone: (1-201) 258-2200
   fax: (1-201) 236-0072
   email: orders@erlbaum.com
   website:www.erlbaum.com

This book explains the development of deaf and hard-of-hearing children in the context of family and school. It shows the role and effects of school environments on development. Each chapter deals with issues of culture and expectations.

Deaf Friendly Pre-Schools and Nurseries (2003, 37 pages)
Anne-Marie Hall and Hilary Sutherland
   National Deaf Children's Society (NDCS)
   15 Dufferin Street
   London EC1Y 8UR, UK
   phone: (44-020) 7490-8656
   fax: (44-020) 7251-5020
   email: ndcs@ndcs.info
   website: www.ndcs.info

Practical guidebook for those working with very young deaf children on how to include deaf children and understand their particular needs. Information for staff in pre-school settings who have a deaf child attending. Covers activities including reading books, group and music time, playing games, and behavior and discipline. Free.

Deaf Friendly Schools: A guide for teachers and governors, with a supplement toolkit on inclusion: Deaf children in mainstream schools (2002, 32 pages)

Clara Ratcliffe
  National Deaf Children's Society (NDCS), UK (see page 241 for address.)

  A guide for staff in mainstream secondary or primary schools who have deaf pupils. Information on teaching strategies, inclusion, communication, deafness, and technical support.

Deaf Like Me (1985, 292 pages)

Thomas S. Spradley and James P. Spradley
  Gallaudet University Press
  Chicago Distribution Center
  11030 South Langley Ave
  Chicago, IL 60628, USA
  phone: (1-773) 568-1550
  phone inside the USA: (1-800) 621-2736
  tty inside the US: (1-888) 630-9347
  fax inside the US: (1-800) 621-8476
  email: kh@press.uchicago.edu
  website: gupress.gallaudet.edu

  Deaf Like Me is an account of parents coming to terms with their baby girl's profound deafness. It expresses the love, hope, and anxieties of many hearing parents of deaf children. In the epilogue, Lynn Spradley as a teenager reflects upon being deaf, her education, her struggle to communicate, and the discovery that she was the focus of her father's and uncle's book.

Deafness: A guide for parents, teachers, and community workers (2001, 32 pages)

Akach Philemon
  Special Needs Education, UNESCO
  7 Place de Fontenoy
  75352 Paris 07-SP, France
  fax: (33-145) 685-627
  email: ie@unesco.org
      k.eklindh@unesco.org
  website: unesdoc.unesco.org/images/
  0012/001255/125541e.pdf

  This short and simply-written UNESCO publication explains many complex issues related to deafness, sign language, and the education of deaf children. It is intended to raise awareness among parents, teachers, doctors, nurses, and social workers of the importance of sign language for deaf children, particularly in the early years. It is accompanied by a video. Free.

Developing Personal Safety Skills in Children with Disabilities (1995, 214 pages)

F. Briggs
  Paul H. Brooks Publishing Co
  PO Box 10624
  Baltimore, MD 21285-0624, USA

  Offers learning activities to develop self-esteem, assertiveness, and independence — skills that children with disabilities need to safeguard themselves. It can be used to teach children to recognize dangerous situations, take action, handle approaches by strangers, communicate their feelings, and to recognize right and wrong ways of touching.

Family Action for Inclusion in Education (2002, 120 pages)

EENET, School of Education
University of Manchester, Oxford Road
Manchester M13 9PL, UK
phone: (44 -161) 275-3711
fax: (44 -161) 275-3548
email: info@eenet.org.uk
website: www.eenet.org.uk

  A practical and inspirational handbook with stories of family-based advocacy organizations that have helped to transform educational systems in southern Africa, South Asia, Europe, and Australia. Useful for family and community members who want to form a support group or challenge exclusion. Provides valuable insights into the activities, thoughts, and feelings of parents involved in fighting for the inclusion of their disabled children.

Hearing Aids: A guide (2003, 52 pages)

National Deaf Children's Society (NDCS), UK
(see address on page 241)

Information about different types of hearing aids, care and maintenance, and simple repairs. Provides a range of information on the different types of hearing aids available. This booklet is aimed at both parents and professionals.

Kid-Friendly Parenting with Deaf and Hard-of-Hearing Children: A treasury of fun activities toward better behavior. (1995, 373 pages)

D. Medwid and D. Chapman-Weston
Gallaudet University Press
(see address on page 242)

This step-by-step guide presents hundreds of ideas and activities for use with children who are deaf or cannot hear well, ages 3 to 12. In addition to short, clear descriptions of parenting techniques, each chapter includes a commentary from deaf and hearing experts. Information is provided about special resources and support services.

Let's Communicate: A handbook for people working with children with communication difficulties
(1997, Ref: WHO/RHB 971)

Co-published by WHO, UNICEF, and Ministry of Health, Zimbabwe
Available free from:
Ms. Sonia Florisses, Disability and Rehabilitation Team
WHO, CH-1211,
Geneva 27, Switzerland
email: florisses@who.ch

This consists of a series of booklets, one of which is about working with children with hearing impairments.

The New Language of Toys: Teaching communication skills to children with special needs (1996, 289 pages)

S. Schwartz and J.E. Heller
Woodbine House
(see address on page 241)

This book provides ideas to parents and professionals about how to use everyday toys to stimulate and promote language development in children with additional needs.

Not Deaf Enough: Raising a child who is hard-of-hearing with hugs and humor (1996, 242 pages)

Morgan Candlish and Patricia Ann
A.G. Bell Association for the Deaf
(see address on page 239)

This book demonstrates a family's support for their youngest child who has a mild-to-moderate hearing loss. His mother explains the challenges that the family faced and conquered together.

Omni-Directory (2003)

National Deaf Children's Society (NDCS), UK
(see address on page 241)

A guide to products and services for families of deaf children, young people, and those professionals working with them.

The Parents' Guide to Cochlear Implants (2002, 168 pages)

Patricia M. Chute and Mary Ellen Nevins
Gallaudet University Press
(see address on page 242)

Make informed decisions about cochlear implants with this easy-to-follow guide.

Preparing Teachers for Inclusion
(1996, video)

EENET
School of Education
(see address on page 242)

This video package from Lesotho features footage of deaf children included in their local schools.

The Psychology of Deafness: Understanding deaf and hard-of-hearing people (1990, 292 pages)

M. Vernon and J.F. Andrews
Longman. White Plains, NY.
UMI: Books On Demand
300 North Zeeb Road
Ann Arbor, MI 48106-1346, USA
phone inside the US: (800) 521-3042
fax: (1-734) 973-1464
email: info@umi.com
website: www.umi.com

This book helps explain how the lives of people who are deaf or cannot hear well are different from the lives of people who can hear. It helps explain the level of stress involved in coping with the world.

Quality Standards in the Early Years: Guidelines on working with deaf children under two years old and their families (2002, 32 pages)

National Deaf Children's Society (NDCS), UK
(see address on page 241)

Gives guidelines for good practices in the education of deaf children, covering the early years, working in partnership, and inclusion.

Raising and Educating a Deaf Child: A comprehensive guide to the choices, controversies, and decisions faced by parents and educators (1999, 256 pages)

Marc Marschark
Oxford University Press
Saxon Way West
Corby, Northants NN18 9ES, UK
email: bookorders.uk@oup.com
website: www.oup.co.uk/bookshop/

Discusses the implications of raising and teaching a child who is deaf or cannot hear well, trying to educate parents so they can make knowledgeable decisions. Covers such topics as medical causes of early hearing loss, language acquisition, social and intellectual development, education, and environment. Includes a phone number and address section on information sources and organizations serving deaf children.

Raising Your Hearing Impaired Child: A guideline for parents (1982, 238 pages)

S.H. McArthur
A.G. Bell Association for the Deaf
(see address on page 239)

Written by a teacher, who is also the mother of two deaf daughters, this book offers ideas and suggestions for parents raising their deaf child using oral methods.

Sign Language (2003, 6 pages)

National Deaf Children's Society (NDCS), UK
(see address on page 241)

A practical guide on learning sign language and how to find out more information.

The Silent Garden: Raising your deaf child (Revised edition, 2002, 304 pages)

P.W. Ogden
Gallaudet University Press
(see address on page 242)

Ogden, who is himself profoundly deaf from birth, provides a foundation for parents to make the difficult decisions necessary to help their deaf child reach full potential.

Speak to Me! (1995, 154 pages)

Marcia Calhoun Forecki
  Gallaudet University Press
  (see address on page 242)

  A down-to-earth account of how a single mother copes with accepting her 18-month-old son's deafness.

Teaching Children to Protect Themselves (2000, 154 pages)

F. Briggs and M. McVeity
  Allen & Unwin
  83 Alexander Street
  Crows Nest NSW 2065, Australia
  phone: (61-2) 8425-0100
  fax: (61-2) 9906-2218
  email: frontdesk@allen-unwin.com.au
  web site: www.allenandunwin.com

  A handbook that offers guidance to teachers and counselors on how to protect young children from sexual abuse. It has many useful activities to help children learn about staying safe.

Understanding Deafness
(2003, 28 pages)

  National Deaf Children's Society
  (NDCS), UK
  (see address on page 241)

  An introductory guide to different types of deafness, hearing tests, audiograms, communication, and language.

When Your Child is Deaf: A guide for parents (2002, 191 pages)

David Luterman and Mark Ross
  York Press, Inc.
  PO Box 594
  Timonium, MD 21094, USA
  phone inside the US: (800) 962-2763
  fax: (1-410) 560-6758
  email: info@yorkpress.com
  website: www.yorkpress.com

  Information, advice, and encouragement for parents about the emotional and educational processes of coming to terms with a hearing impairment in their child.

You and Your Deaf Child: A self-help guide for parents of deaf and hard-of-hearing children (1998, 240 pages)

John Adams
  Gallaudet University Press
  (see address on page 242)

  This down-to-earth book focuses on feelings about hearing loss, the importance of communication in the family, and effective behavior management. Many chapters contain practical activities and questions to help parents learn new skills. Appendices include references, general resources, checklists, and guidelines for evaluating educational programs.

The Young Deaf Child (1999, 214 pages)

David M. Luterman and others
  York Press, Inc.
  (see address at left)

  This book provides information to guide caregivers in raising a deaf child when hearing loss is discovered. It presents historical information plus the choices that are available so that parents can decide what is right for their family. The authors recognize that each family is different and has their own needs, so no one method is advocated over another.

Other Books from the Hesperian Foundation

Helping Children Who Are Blind, by Sandy Niemann and Namita Jacob, aids parents and other caregivers in helping blind children develop all their capabilities. Topics include: assessing what a child can see, preventing blindness, moving around safely, teaching common activities, and more. 192 pages.

Disabled Village Children, by David Werner, covers most common disabilities of children. It gives suggestions for rehabilitation at the village level and explains how to make a variety of appropriate, low-cost aids. Emphasis is placed on how to help disabled children find a role and be accepted in the community. 672 pages.

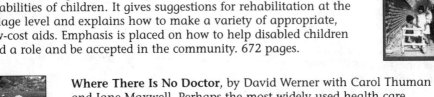

Where There Is No Doctor, by David Werner with Carol Thuman and Jane Maxwell. Perhaps the most widely used health care manual in the world, this book provides vital, easily understood information on how to diagnose, treat and prevent common diseases. Emphasis is placed on prevention, including cleanliness, diet, and vaccinations, as well as the active role people must take in their own health care. 512 pages.

Where There Is No Dentist, by Murray Dickson, shows people how to care for their own teeth and gums, and how to prevent tooth and gum problems through hygiene, nutrition, and education, in the home, community, and school. This book gives detailed, well illustrated information on using dental equipment, placing fillings, taking out teeth, and more. A new chapter includes material on HIV/AIDS and oral health. 237 pages.

Helping Health Workers Learn, by David Werner and Bill Bower. An indispensable resource for teaching about health, this heavily illustrated book makes health education fun and effective. Includes activities for mothers and children; pointers for using theater, flannel-boards, and other techniques; and many ideas for producing low-cost teaching aids. This people-centered approach presents strategies for effective community involvement through participatory education. 640 pages.

A Book for Midwives, by Susan Klein, is for midwives, community health workers and anyone concerned about pregnant women and their babies. An invaluable tool for training as well as a practical reference, the author covers helping pregnant women stay healthy; care and complications during labor, childbirth and after birth; family planning; breastfeeding; and homemade, low-cost equipment. 528 pages.

Where Women Have No Doctor, by A. August Burns, Ronnie Lovich, Jane Maxwell, and Katharine Shapiro, combines self-help medical information with an understanding of the ways poverty, discrimination, and cultural beliefs limit women's health and access to care. An essential resource on the problems that affect only women or that affect women differently from men. 584 pages.